Web Site Usability:

A Designer's Guide

The Morgan Kaufmann Series in Interactive Technologies

Series Editors: Stuart Card, Xerox PARC; Jonathan Grudin, University of California, Irvine; Mark Linton, Vitria Technology; Jakob Nielsen, Nielsen Norman Group; Tim Skelly, Design Happy

Web Site Usability: A Designer's Guide
Jared M. Spool, Tara Scanlon, Will Schroeder, Carolyn Snyder, and Terri DeAngelo

The Usability Engineering Lifecycle
Deborah Mayhew

Readings in Information Visualization: Using Vision to Think
Edited by Stuart Card, Jock Mackinlay, and Ben Shneiderman

The Design of Children's Technology
Edited by Allison Druin

Contextual Design: Defining Customer-Centered Systems
Hugh Beyer and Karen Holztblatt

Human-Computer Interface Design: Success Stories, Emerging Methods, and Real-World Context
Edited by Marianne Rudisill, Clayton Lewis, Peter Polson, and Timothy McKay

Web Site Usability:

A Designer's Guide

Jared M. Spool

PRINCIPAL INVESTIGATOR

Tara Scanlon   Carolyn Snyder

Will Schroeder   Terri DeAngelo

USER INTERFACE ENGINEERING

Morgan Kaufmann Publishers, Inc.
San Francisco, California

Senior Editor   Diane D. Cerra
Director of Production and Manufacturing   Yonie Overton
Assistant Production Manager   Julie Pabst
Proofreader   Jennifer McClain
File Preparation   Technologies 'N Typography
Cover Design   Ross Carron Design
Cover Image   Arthur Tress/Photonica
Printer   Courier Corporation

This book was typeset in PageMaker by the authors.

Designations used by companies to distinguish their products are often claimed as trademarks or registered trademarks. In all instances where Morgan Kaufmann Publishers, Inc. is aware of a claim, the product names appear in initial capital or all capital letters. Readers, however, should contact the appropriate companies for more complete information regarding trademarks and registration.

Morgan Kaufmann Publishers, Inc.
Editorial and Sales Office
340 Pine Street, Sixth Floor
San Francisco, CA 94104-3205
USA
Telephone 415/392-2665
Facsimile 415/982-2665
Email mkp@mkp.com
WWW http://www.mkp.com

Library of Congress Cataloging-in-Publication Data

Spool, Jared M.
    Web site usability : a designer's guide / Jared M. Spool . . . [et al.].
        p.   cm.—(The Morgan Kaufmann series in interactive technologies)
    ISBN 1-55860-569-X
    1. Web sites—Design.; f=oc. I. Title. II. Series.
TK5105.888.S72   1999
005.7'2—dc21   98-53859
                                                 CIP

In loving memory
Liz Cowan
1959-1996

Contents

Part 2: Site Scrapbook

Part 3: Testing Sites

Preface

Just as we were putting the finishing touches on this report, I got a call from an old friend who does web site design for a major corporation.

"So Jared," he said, "I hear you guys did this big study about web sites."

"Yeah," I replied. "We watched a whole bunch of people doing informational searches, trying to look up specific facts and stuff. It was absolutely fascinating! In fact, I'll bet you lunch that you can't tell me what we found. I'll give you three guesses."

"Free food? You're on!" My friend thought a moment. "Well, I imagine a consistent navigational structure was probably pretty important. Right now at work, we're trying to develop a shell for our entire site, so the individual departments just supply content."

"Nope, that wasn't it," I said. "In fact, we tested a couple of sites that took a shell approach, where the high-level links stayed the same whenever the underlying content changed. I hate to say it, but they didn't do very well. People had a hard time finding anything. It seems that you can't really separate content and navigation without losing something important in the process."

"Huh, no kidding. That's not good news," my friend sighed. "Well, let's see... I bet part of it had to do with graphics — like good graphic design, the right colors, and all that."

I searched for the right words, because among his other skills, my friend is a talented graphic designer. "Ah, no, sorry. We measured all kinds of graphical aspects, and nothing really makes a difference one way or the other. The best thing we can say about graphics is that, most of the time, they don't do much harm. Oh, except for animation — that really annoys people."

There was a longer silence this time. "Well, at least tell me that good page layout was important."

I cringed, because I knew I'd disappoint him again. "We actually found just the opposite. Page layout, at least as it's traditionally defined, needs to be different for the web. For example, sites with lots of white-space did worst. And the same thing for readability — sites that were 'readable' by conventional measures seemed to make it harder to find information."

"Come on Jared, you're making even less sense than usual. Are you telling me that everything I know about web site design is wrong?"

"No, no, relax," I assured him. "It's not that bad. The bottom line for web design is still to provide useful content in a format that works the way people think. It's just that, in the course of our research, we saw a lot of sites doing things that get in the way of that. Now that we've had a chance to look at the data, we think we have some insight into at least some of the problems."

"Okay, now I'm hooked," he said. "Why don't I buy you that lunch sometime next week, and you can give me the scoop?"

I smiled as I pulled out my calendar. It would be an interesting lunch!

Purpose of This Report

This report isn't about the theory of web site design. It's based on data from our research, and describes how well (and poorly) some information-rich web sites actually work when people use them to find specific answers.

We realize that we probably weren't using these sites in the way that their designers intended. We ignored most of the sales and marketing issues, and have no data on how well any of these sites meet their intended purposes. In fact, based on our study, we can't say whether a site's design is good or bad overall. We only know what happened when people tried to find information.

We certainly don't know everything about web site design. Since this was an exploratory study, subsequent research on web site usability may weaken or even contradict our findings. This report shares what we found, and what we think it means. We'll also give you some ways to evaluate and improve the usability of your own web site for information-finding tasks. But no one should accept our reasoning without question. For your site, do your own testing... and let us know what you find!

Acknowledgments

This report is the culmination of a lot of hard work by many people. Without them, my dream of conducting groundbreaking research on web site usability would have remained just that — a dream.

Throughout this report, you'll see the term "we" frequently ("We saw...," "We think..."). Because this project was such a collaborative effort, it's impossible to tell where one person's thoughts end and another's begin. Although this was a group effort, I want to acknowledge the contributions of several key players.

Will Schroeder was instrumental in designing the study and analyzing the results. Will is our statistical wizard who specializes in small data sets. Without Will's analysis, this report would be just a collection of anecdotes.

This whole project wouldn't have happened without Terri DeAngelo, a fellow from the Massachusetts Software Council Fellowship Program. Terri's research background was invaluable to us. She assisted with the design of the study, conducted most of the usability tests, analyzed copious amounts of data, and painstakingly documented her observations. We wish her success in her future endeavors.

Tara Scanlon had just started at our company when we were considering this research, so she designed and conducted the pilot study. Based on those results, we had a better idea of what to look for in the actual research.

Once we completed the study, we had binders full of usability test logs and extensive spreadsheets containing our analysis. Carolyn Snyder worked with Tara to do the writing, editing, fact-checking, screen capturing, layout, and proof-reading necessary to transform our really cool scientific findings into coherent prose and illustrations. Richard Danca, another of our SCFP fellows, assisted with the editing and proofing.

Our office staff — Cheryl Whitney, Heather Byrne, and Enid Colon — deserve our thanks for their help with the logistics of user scheduling and for putting up with the insanity involved in producing a book-length report.

Last but not least, thanks to our users for providing the data. Their struggles, feedback, and insights are the foundation for this report.

— *Jared Spool*
June 1997

Part 1:
Research Results

Everyone has opinions about what makes a good web site. Web site navigation, links, graphic design, page layout, and user satisfaction have all been discussed in the popular press ad nauseam.

Our research, however, provides actual data — not opinions — about what makes web sites usable. You may be surprised at some of our findings. We certainly were!

The chapters in Part 1 present the most interesting findings from our research. We don't have all the answers about how to design a usable web site, but we're starting to learn where some of the problems with current web site design lie.

As an industry, we have a long way to go.

CHAPTER 1

Web Site Usability: The Big Picture

A year ago, we started wondering what made a web site usable. We had heard the opinions of experienced designers about what they felt it took to create a good site. We looked at books and magazines that talked about how to make a "cool" site. But no matter where we looked, we couldn't find any data — based on real user experience — about what it takes to make a *usable* site.

This report is our attempt to start providing that data to web site designers.

What Is "Usability" on the Web?

We set out to study usability of web sites, but we first had to determine what that means. The usability of a site depends on what users are trying to accomplish. Are they surfing?

Doing research? Buying products? Downloading software? And it also depends on the organization's goals for creating the web site. Is the site aimed at marketing a service? Selling merchandise? Making information available to employees, shareholders, and customers?

Whatever the goal, *information* is a central theme. For intranets (internal web sites), information is *the* theme — no one surfs the online employee policy manual just for kicks. Because of this, we focused our study on how successful sites are at providing people with information so they can make decisions. The more a site helps people find the information they are looking for, the more usable it is.

The Sites We Tested

We picked a set of nine popular sites with content we thought would be useful for a general audience, as shown in Table 1.1. Two of the sites, Disney and C|net, were high-profile sites that had been well-reviewed by the media. We expected that these sites would do the best, and that we could learn from them about successful web site design.

True to the ever-changing nature of the web, two of the sites were updated in the middle of our study. The Disney site changed to a frame-based design, and the layout of Inc.'s home page also changed. We collected enough data to include both versions in our findings. To our dismay, the Olympic site (which had done well in our study) disappeared before we could obtain screen shots for this report.

Site Name	Content
C|net www.cnet.com	Technology resources and information, product reviews, listings of where to buy products.
Disney www.disney.com	Games, videos, merchandise, Disneyland and Walt Disney World theme park information and reservations.
Edmund's www.edmunds.com	Car and truck prices, specifications, reviews, and other resources for vehicle buyers
Fidelity www.fidelity.com	Fidelity mutual funds, personal and corporate investing opportunities.
Hewlett Packard www.hp.com	Product information, financial information, job opportunities.
Inc. www.inc.com	Small business resources, book reviews, articles, conferences, contact information for organizations.
Olympics (No longer available)	Schedules and results from the 1996 Olympic summer games in Atlanta, merchandise, tickets.
Travelocity www.travelocity.com	Airline tickets, car and hotel reservations, guide to recreational activities worldwide.
WebSaver www.websaver.com	Annuity information.

TABLE 1.1

We studied nine different web sites. Two of them, Inc. and Disney, were redesigned in the middle of the study.

"Scavenger Hunt" Tests

All these sites, while obviously trying to sell products, also provide information. Because we wanted to learn how easy it was for users to answer questions on these sites, we set up a "scavenger hunt" usability test.

We brought in users who were familiar with a web browser, sat them down in front of a site, and watched them try to answer four types of questions, as described in Table 1.2. They had to hunt through the site to find the answer, even if they already knew it. We wanted to see how they searched and what factors of the site helped or hindered them.

TABLE 1.2

We asked users four types of questions at each site. We told them it was possible to answer the questions without leaving the site.

Type of Question	Examples
Simple Facts	Is there any place to go horseback riding on the north shore of Boston? (Travelocity) Can you get a Honda Accord for under $15,000? (Edmund's)
Comparison of Facts	Which is cheaper to fly to, Nevada or England? (Travelocity) Which has better acceleration, the Jeep Cherokee or the Toyota Land Cruiser? (Edmund's)
Judgment	Would you like to go on a day trip to Hampton Court? (Travelocity) Do you think a used Ford F-10 is safe enough? (Edmund's)
Comparison of Judgment	Which show would you like to go to in London with your nine-year old niece? (Travelocity) Which convertible is the best deal for under $20,000? (Edmund's)

The Results

Searching for information on web sites is an intensely frustrating experience. Throughout our study, we were amazed by the time and effort it took users to answer even simple questions. And repeatedly, users gave up without ever finding what they were looking for. Even in the smaller web sites, we watched users get lost or wander off the site without being aware of it.

The Rankings

After more than 50 tests, we have a good idea of how our sites compare to each other. The results are startling. Disney and C|net — the sites we expected to do best — fared poorly in our study. Edmund's, which none of us would have bet on, came in first. Figure 1.1 shows how the sites compared.

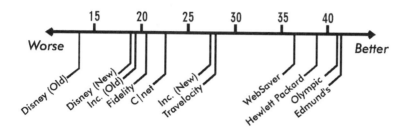

FIGURE 1.1

The relative rankings of the nine sites in our study, based on how successful users were at finding information.

Room for Improvement

Comparing the sites to each other tells only part of the story. Even Edmund's, the best site in our study, fell far short of the highest possible score. Clearly, when it comes to web site design, there is room for improvement.

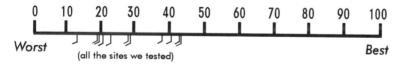

FIGURE 1.2

The entire scale, illustrating how much room there is for improvement in web site usability.

For designers, this is actually good news. Many people we've talked to know that their sites have usability problems, but don't know where to look to begin fixing them. In the course of our research, we gained some insight into which aspects of site design can help or hinder users the most.

Beyond the Rankings

After looking at the site rankings, our ideas about successful web site design were turned completely upside-down. To find out why, we began scrutinizing the sites themselves, looking for similarities and differences that might account for the users' success or lack thereof. We used a statistical model to discover which factors were most correlated with user success.

There were lots of surprises. When we found things that flew in the face of common sense and the recommendations of other designers, we did more tests to get more data. We even conducted some parts of the analysis two or three different ways, and got the same results.

Later chapters describe our findings in detail. But first, let's look at some of the high-level implications of these results.

The Major Implications

Some of the results of our study are counterintuitive, but what makes our research both controversial and fascinating are its implications. These results could dramatically change the way people develop web pages.

Implication 1:
Graphic Design Neither Helps Nor Hurts

As hard as we looked, we couldn't find any evidence that graphic design helps users retrieve information from a site.

Consider the following:

- We measured all the graphic design elements we could think of, and none of them had any significant correlation — either positive or negative — with users' success (for more information, see Chapter 7, Graphic Design on the Web).

- Several of the sites had very professional-looking designs. The Hewlett Packard and Olympics sites did well, while C|net and Disney — also graphically intense — scored at the lower end of our ratings.

- Edmund's, the top-scoring site in our study, is mostly text.

- When users navigated, they often tried text links first, ignoring nearby graphics.

Of course, graphics may be important in other ways, such as for conveying marketing messages, making users more willing to return to the site, or selling products. We didn't measure these, so we don't know. But as far as we can tell, graphic design is completely unrelated to success at finding information on web sites.

Implication 2:
Text Links Are Vital

In watching users work with the sites, we couldn't help notice how important text links are. Because of downloading delays, text links are often the first things visible on the page. Most users examined text links before considering image links.

There are many different types and styles of links, and some styles do seem to work better than others (for more information, see Chapter 3, Getting Around: Links). More important than style, however, is the predictiveness of the link. The better users could predict where a link would lead, the more successful they were in finding information.

The text link is the way users prefer to navigate sites. Yet, very little of the design advice available talks about how to create effective text links. This is clearly an area for further study.

Implication 3:
Navigation and Content Are Inseparable

We've heard a lot about the *shell strategy* — a technique that lets developers design a navigational structure and hierarchy first, then just plug the content into it. For example, one of our clients (a large multinational bank) has one department working on the overall look and feel of the site, including the home page, navigation bars, style sheets, and templates for different types of interactions. Other departments are responsible for creating the content. The developers of the overall structure — or shell — don't know what the content will be because it will be plugged in later.

When we were doing our research, we didn't talk with any of the site developers, but saw a few shell sites nonetheless. (Our rule of thumb for identifying shells is this: If you could remove more than half of the site content without having to update the home page, it's most likely a shell site.) Inc.'s home page is one example, as shown in Figure 1.3. The links are so generic that users rarely got what they expected.

BEYOND THE MAGAZINE

Articles and interviews available only online: _Inc. Real Time_, _Zinc_, _Online Entrepreneur_, and _Between the Pages_.

VIRTUAL CONSULTANT

Try out our interactive worksheets and searchable databases. Visit the reference desk, software libraries, bulletin boards, and Web links. Create your own Web site.

INC. MAGAZINE

Read the current issue and _Inc._'s archives (over 5,000 articles). Information about _Inc._, Inc. Online, and subscriptions. The _Inc. 500_ area.

INC. BUSINESS RESOURCES

Inc. products, conferences, and consulting services. The Positive Performer customer service awards. Inc.World Boston and San Diego expos.

FIGURE 1.3

This detail from Inc.'s home page shows how it fits our definition of a "shell site," because it contains so many generic links.

Based on our observations of Inc. and other shell sites, we have no evidence to suggest that the shell strategy can succeed. The sites that were most successful were those where content and navigation were inextricably linked — where you couldn't remove content without updating all of the main navigation pages.

The problem with shells is that by definition they require lots of generic links, which make it harder for users to predict what they will find. This implication makes development of large web sites significantly more difficult, because it suggests that the home page and high-level links may need to change more frequently.

Implication 4: Information Retrieval Is Different than Surfing

Our study focused on one specific activity: information retrieval within a large site. We didn't study surfing, the other primary use of web sites. When users surf, they are just browsing, clicking whatever looks most interesting or "cool," and content may not be the driving force in coolness.

In the movie *Wayne's World*, there is a scene where Wayne opens a door in a local donut shop to reveal a troupe of black-clad warriors practicing martial arts. He watches them for a moment and then shuts the door, proclaiming "I've always wanted to open a door and see a bunch of guys Kung-Fu fighting." The scene is completely irrelevant to the rest of the movie — it's just cool. When users surf the web, they're looking for the guys who are Kung-Fu fighting.

When looking for information, users are much more focused. They tend to click on the link most likely to yield the information they're hunting for. The kinds of things designers put on web sites to attract surfing users proved to be distractions during information retrieval tasks. For example, users saw advertisements as visual "noise," and animation was so irritating that some users covered it up!

This implies that sites aimed at information retrieval need to be designed differently from sites aimed at surfing. These are conflicting goals. Unfortunately, we don't yet have all the answers about where the differences lie.

Implication 5: Web Sites Aren't Like Software

Companies have been usability testing their software products for years. Our firm alone has conducted thousands of usability tests on hundreds of software and hardware products. We've learned a lot about measuring usability. We assumed that the web sites would just be another form of software, and could be tested similarly.

Boy, were we wrong! The web presents lots of problems that we've never seen before, which make it hard to define what usability even is, let alone measure it.

Consider user preference. When we do comparative testing, we ask users which product they like the most after they've worked with all of them. Almost without fail, users choose the same product that they were most successful with. For software, we've found that user preference can be a reasonably good proxy for measuring usability.

This is not true for web sites. We asked users to pick which site they liked the best. While some people chose the site they were most successful with, others did not. These users liked a site because of its content, rather than the site's ability to help them find information. They'd say things like "I liked Disney, it seemed more interesting," even if they had gotten completely lost and failed to complete any of the tasks.

For web sites, user preference obviously doesn't measure the same things it does for software, so our tried-and-true proxy suddenly doesn't work any more. And the more data we find, the more we realize we don't really know what makes a web site usable.

The web is a whole new ball game, and we're still learning how to play. We don't yet know how to design for finding information. We don't know how to design for comparisons so that users can find the best house, car, or job — things the press tells us the web excels at. We don't know how to effectively use multiple media like graphics, animation, interactive applets, and text to produce the best results.

To web site designers, this probably doesn't feel like good news. But with this study we now have some insights we never had before, and we hope that our results will inspire further research into all these areas.

CHAPTER 2

Getting Around: Navigation

Like most aspects of usability, navigation is invisible when it's working. But when there's a problem, users can get completely stuck. In fact, navigation problems frequently caused users to give up.

The problems we saw were primarily due to two things:

- Users did not have the domain — or business area — knowledge they needed to navigate the site

- The site structure didn't meet users' expectations

We also looked at some of the devices that designers used to help users traverse their sites: frames, tables of contents, and so on. (We looked at links also, and found that they deserve their own chapter. For more information, see Chapter 3.) Some of these devices helped, and some didn't. You might want to check them out before you put lots of effort into implementing them for your site.

Domain Knowledge and Navigation

Some of the sites we tested, such as Travelocity and Fidelity, assumed that users had a lot of detailed knowledge about the domain — or business area — covered by the site. These sites tended to finish low in our ratings because users didn't have the knowledge they needed. When users aren't familiar with the domain, they don't understand the options that are presented to them.

High-ranking sites such as Hewlett Packard and Edmund's did not assume domain knowledge. In fact, where there was possible confusion, these sites put in explicit navigational cues. Let's look at some examples.

The Domain of Travel

The 3 Best Itineraries section of the Travelocity site (see Figure 2.1) appears to be designed from a travel agent's point of view. The system expected users to enter a round-trip destination (Boston to London, then London to Boston). However, several users tried to compare two flights to two *different* locations at the same time, such as Boston to Las Vegas and Boston to London. To these users, having multiple fields implied they could enter different information.

The site assumed that users understand the basic paradigm of booking travel. Users didn't realize that they were booking segments of a trip, most likely because of the terminology. The term *segments* is familiar to a travel agent but had little meaning to most users, who thought in terms of round-trips.

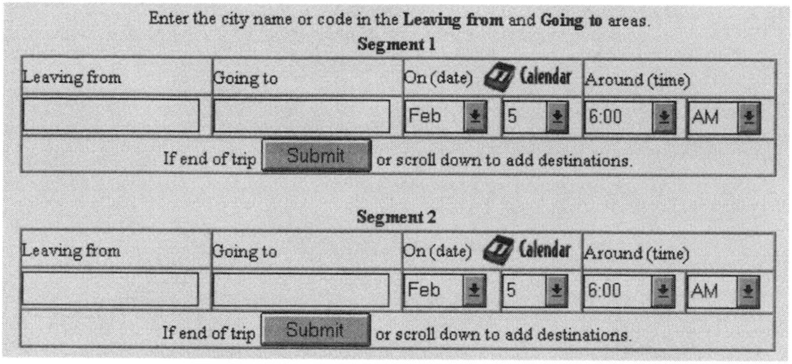

FIGURE 2.1

Many users didn't understand the concept of a "segment."

Recently, the Travelocity site was changed to include a "Round Trip" check box, as shown in Figure 2.2. No one has had problems with the concept of segments since this change was made.

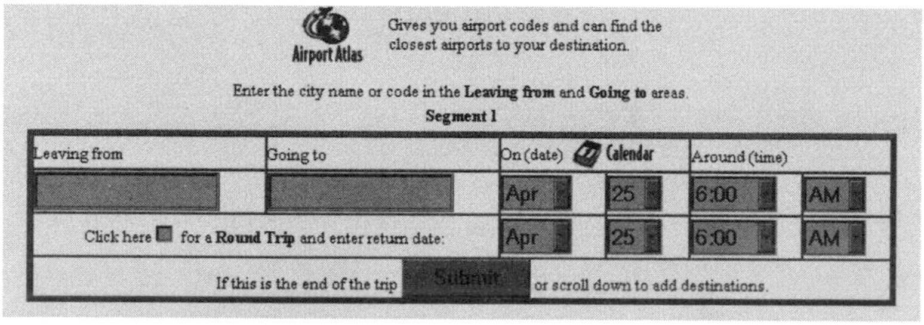

FIGURE 2.2

No one has had trouble with the concept of "segments" since the Round Trip check box was added.

The Investment Domain

The Fidelity site assumes that users are knowledgeable about investing. When users were searching, they had to specify which parts of the site to search, as shown in Figure 2.3. Unfortunately, most users couldn't determine whether they should search Fidelity Mutual Funds, Fidelity Daily NAVs, or Personal Investing. In fact, users couldn't explain the differences among these three categories. In this case, a lack of domain knowledge made the site unsearchable for them.

FIGURE 2.3

Users of the Fidelity site had to chose which of three areas they wanted to search. Unfortunately, most users didn't know the difference among the three.

The Automotive Domain: Linking Content and Navigation

The Edmund's site does a better job of linking content and navigation. Several users did not know whether a Jeep Grand Cherokee was a car or a truck. The site designers had anticipated this confusion, however, and included a link on the New Cars page saying "For New Pickup, Van and Sport Utility prices, click here!" as shown in Figure 2.4. Because content and navigation were developed together, users were more successful with the site.

FIGURE 2.4

Users who mistakenly went to the New Cars page of the Edmund's site had a quick escape route because the content and navigation were tied together.

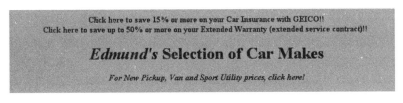

Click here to save 15% or more on your Car Insurance with GEICO!!
Click here to save up to 50% or more on your Extended Warranty (extended service contract)!!

Edmund's **Selection of Car Makes**

For New Pickup, Van and Sport Utility prices, click here!

Web Sites May Have Different Users

We think some of these domain issues arose because the designer assumed the site user was the same as the user for the company's flagship product or service. But this may not be the case — web site users may be different than typical users of the product.

For example, Travelocity is produced by Sabre, the same company that creates the reservation systems used by trained travel agents. Fidelity's software products are used by investment-savvy individuals and professionals. The readers of Inc. magazine are business owners and entrepreneurs. In all these cases, the typical user of the product knows a particular domain. But the web site audience may be quite different from the audience the company usually designs for.

This is only a theory — we didn't talk to the site designers, and the users we tested may be different from the population the site was intended for. However, the fact that Travelocity now supports the concept of round trips suggests that the Travelocity designers may have come to the same realization.

The Structure of Sites

"A well-defined structure... provides users with an obvious, clear model of the information space."

— Darrell Sano
Designing Large-Scale Web Sites

When we started looking for sites to test, one thing we looked for was sites that used different navigational structures. We thought that there *must* be one structure that would work better for users than others. Perhaps a star structure would work, or maybe a sequential structure would be best. Surprisingly, however, we found that the structure of the site made little difference in whether users would be successful.

Users Don't Form Mental Models of Sites

In software applications, users form mental models of the product — how it works and where the functionality is located. We expected that users of web sites would do the same thing: they'd form a mental map of how the site is laid out and how the information is organized. If users did map out the site, we would expect them to use the browser's Go menu if they got lost to quickly get back to a known point. Because they had a mental map, they could return to the point where they made a wrong turn and try a different route.

But none of our users did this. When they got lost, they went forward from where they were, navigating "in the moment." They often could not tell us what the problem was or where they had gone wrong. We didn't see any evidence that users ever attempted to understand the layout of the site. Users apparently don't think about site structure at all. Instead, they continue on an exploratory path through the site until they find what they're looking for or become so frustrated that they give up.

Content and Navigation: Shells

Many of the books about web design imply that you can design a navigational structure and hierarchy — sometimes called a shell — and then just plug the content into it. But after watching users struggle with content and navigation issues, we feel these are so closely intertwined that attempting to separate them will lead to a less effective design.

The reason has to do with the links. By definition, the links used in a shell structure are generic so the underlying content can be modified or added to without changing the high-level structure. Unfortunately, these less-descriptive links made it harder for users to decide what path to pursue. (For more information about links, see Chapter 3, Getting Around: Links.) And if it's true that users navigate in the moment, they may not ever really learn the structure of the site, making every search for information a new guessing game.

Subsites

Users got lost most often in the Disney sites. We believe the problem has to do with the structure. Disney has both a main site and several subsites, as shown in Figure 2.5. Users had different expectations from the site designers of where "home" would take them.

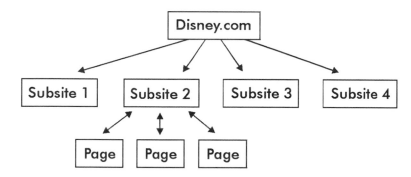

FIGURE 2.5

Users could navigate from the home page to the subsites, but unless they used the Back button or knew the magic link, they couldn't get back home.

Notice that from the main site, disney.com, users could get to the subsites, but unless they were willing to use their browser's Back button or could find the magic link, they could not return. (In the old Disney site, the magic link was a set of mouse ears in the upper corner of the page.)

If users were on a page in a subsite and clicked the home link, they would return to the subsite's home page, not disney.com's home page. In fact, we had several users who were lost in the Disneyland subsite, because they could not get to the Walt Disney World subsite where the answers were.

Devices for Navigation

We also looked at some of the tools, techniques, and tricks that site designers used to help users navigate. Some of these devices were more successful than others.

Device: Frames

Frames, an HTML construct for dividing the browser window into several areas that can scroll and otherwise act independently, have a reputation for causing usability problems. Each frame can display different documents, thus it's possible to change the content of one area without changing the entire window. Many sites use frames to help with navigation, putting a small frame on one side with a table of contents, and a larger frame next to it, where the content is displayed.

Only two of the sites we tested used frames, but the issues we saw were not as significant as we expected them to be. In fact, we were lucky enough to test two versions of the Disney site. The old version did not use frames, but the new one did, as shown in Figure 2.6. The small pane on the right side is a table of contents. Users could click on something in that pane and it would appear in the larger left pane. Thus the table of contents frame was always visible.

Users performed significantly better with the new site than they did with the old. There were other changes to the site as well, so we can't credit the improvement to frames alone. But, as far as we can tell, frames did not hurt the new Disney design.

FIGURE 2.6

The new version of the Disney site used frames: ① is the main content area, ② is the main table of contents, and ③ controls what's listed in the table of contents. As far as we can tell, frames did not hurt the site.

That's not to say that frames are problem-free. One of the main drawbacks we saw pertains to the subtle changes when one frame scrolls to new content.

On the Fidelity site, shown in Figure 2.7, when the user clicked an item in the left frame, the text frame would scroll to that section. However, users didn't always notice that something on the screen had changed so they'd click again. Several users thought the server was down because it didn't seem to respond to their input. This was less of an issue when there was an image on the screen, because the change was more obvious than when it was just text. We didn't see this problem with the Disney site, where the change in the large frame is also quite obvious.

FIGURE 2.7

When users clicked on an item in the left frame of the Fidelity site, they didn't always realize that the content of the large frame had changed.

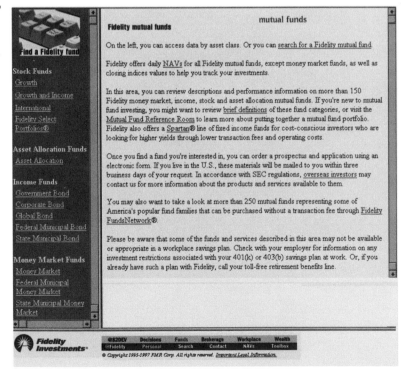

Device: Table of Contents

A table of contents is (usually) a hierarchical listing of the items in the site. Several sites used a table of contents as a navigational device.

The Edmund's home page itself is organized as a table of contents, as shown in Figure 2.8. As with a book, users could look at the home page and know what they would find in each section. Notice that the table of contents also has main categories and subcategories, much like book chapters.

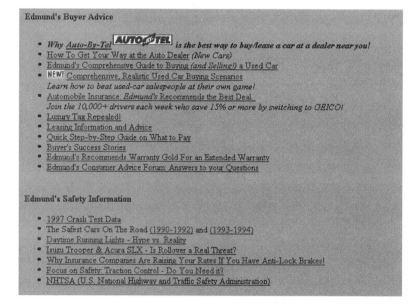

FIGURE 2.8

The Edmund's home page is organized as a table of contents.

Both versions of the Disney site provided a table of contents. In the new Disney site, the right-hand frame functions as a high-level table of contents. There is also a table of contents that is organized like a traditional index in a book, as shown in Figure 2.9. The entries are hierarchical, but organized in alphabetical order. The table of contents is several pages long, and quite detailed. A couple of users navigated the site successfully using the table of contents, though many others ignored it.

FIGURE 2.9

The table of contents on the new Disney site is organized alphabetically.

DISNEY.COM
    E-mail
    Help
        Applications
        Audio
        Error Messages
        Frequently Asked Questions
        Getting Around
        Passwords
        Pictures
        Shopping
        Video
    Registration
    Star Watch
        101 Dalmatians
        Pocahontas
        The Hunchback of Notre Dame
        The Lion King
        Toy Story
        Winnie the Pooh

                                            [Top of Contents]

DISNEY CHANNEL
    Featured Shows
        A Dinosaur's Story
        An American Tail
        Angels in the Outfield
        Audubon's Animal Adventures
        Flash Forward
        Goof Troop
        Heavyweights

Device: Navigation Bars

Sites with navigation buttons or links at the top and bottom of pages did slightly better than sites with navigation buttons down the side of the page. For example, the Hewlett

Packard site has a navigation bar at both the top and bottom of each page. Figure 2.10 shows the bottom buttons.

FIGURE 2.10

Hewlett Packard puts navigation buttons at the top of the site, and repeats selected buttons at the bottom.

We're not exactly sure why navigation bars at the top and bottom are better than navigation at the side, but we have some hypotheses. First, side navigation bars are subject to scrolling problems. Users can scroll them off the screen, or lose context because they only see part of the navigation bar.

Also, users seem to want to use navigation bars after they've determined that the page won't give them what they need. That's often after they've scrolled to the top or bottom of the page. It's very convenient to have a navigation bar staring them in the face at that point.

Device: Hierarchical Maps

Several users got confused because they didn't know exactly where they were in the site's hierarchy. For example, the Olympic site used an imagemap as table of contents for the site, with scaled-down versions of the map as a navigational aid at the top of each page, as shown in Figure 2.11. Some users were confused by these second-level maps. They clicked on the map section they were already in, which in some cases took them several levels up in the hierarchy.

FIGURE 2.11

The Olympic site put a navigational imagemap at the top of the page. Because there's no good indication of where users are in the site, they often clicked on the section they were already in.

The imagemap did not visually indicate which section users were currently in. Text links generally change color after they've been visited, but this image did not. We wonder whether a more explicit "You are here" indicator might have alleviated this problem.

This problem provides additional evidence for our theory that users don't form mental site maps. If they did, they'd know where they were at any given moment.

Device: "You Are Here"

The C|net site attempted to help users keep track of where they were in the hierarchy. Each page included a series of connected buttons, as shown in Figure 2.12. The first button was the top level of the hierarchy, and subsequent buttons listed the other levels. We expected that this would help people track where they were, but only one user gave any indication of seeing it.

FIGURE 2.12

The C|net site used buttons to show users where they were in the hierarchy and to help them get back to higher levels. The user is currently in the comparative reviews ② section of reviews ①.

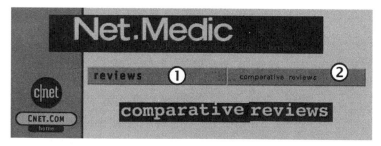

Device: Site Maps

Site maps are visual representations of the content of the site. The only site we tested that had a site map was Fidelity, as shown in Figure 2.13. The users who used Fidelity's site map were twice as successful at finding answers on that site as the users who did not. While we don't have enough data to recommend that all sites have maps, it might be worth investigating further.

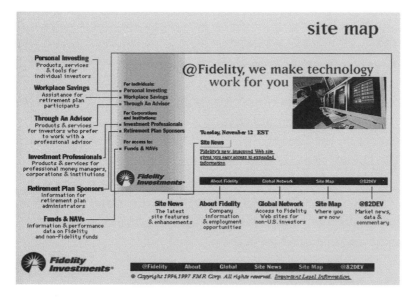

Figure 2.13

Users who used the Fidelity site map were twice as likely to be successful as those who didn't. We think this is because the site map clarifies where the links will lead.

We believe this site map works because it gives users more information about where the links lead. For more details about the importance of understandable links, see Chapter 3, Getting Around: Links.

User Navigation Tactics

In the course of our testing, we saw some tactical patterns in the way people navigated while looking for information.

Note that these categories are not mutually exclusive; users often tried several different tactics.

Searching

About one-third of our users always tried to answer questions by going to the site's search facility. A couple of sites didn't have a search tool, and we saw one user give up on a site because of this. Also, this tactic did not always lead to success, given the problems discussed in Chapter 4, Within-Site Searching.

Just the FAQs

Another tactic users tried was going to the site's Frequently Asked Questions (FAQ) list. In general, this was effective except on the Disney site. Unlike the other sites we tested, the Disney site gave you a different FAQ depending on where you were in the site. So if a user was in Help and requested the FAQ, the site returned a list of the frequently asked questions about Help. This puzzled users — they only expected one FAQ per site.

The Back Button

Many people used the browser Back button to go back one or two pages. Interestingly, if something was further back, most users would try to use the page navigation to get there instead.

Several users didn't use the Back button at all. We think they either didn't know about it or forgot it. They occasionally ran into trouble when they went to a page that had no links off it. To get unstuck, they used the bookmark we had created to the home page and started over from scratch.

Backing Up to Advance

In some instances, users returned to the site's home page to choose a link, even though that same link was available on the page they were on. We aren't sure why they did this, but it might be because they remembered seeing the link on the home page.

We've also seen users exhibit similar behavior when testing other types of software. Starting from a known place may help keep users from getting lost, or at least that's their perception.

CHAPTER 3

Getting Around: Links

Links are closely tied to navigation. While navigation refers to the structure of the site and the patterns by which users traverse the site, links are the mechanism by which they move from one place to another. Successful link structures can help users navigate the site more effectively.

During our testing, we learned that the success of a link depends on:

- How well the user can *predict* where the link will lead.
- How well the user can *differentiate* one link from other, nearby links.

We also learned that link layout and where links lead can affect user success.

Two Extremes: A Comparison of Links

Let's start by looking at two sites that use very different approaches to links: Edmund's and Disney. Edmund's did significantly better than Disney in our study, and links may have been one reason.

At one end of the spectrum, the Edmund's site uses long text links in a bulleted single-column format, as shown in Figure 3.1. Notice that the site designers even added a sentence of descriptive text when the link wasn't clear enough.

FIGURE 3.1

The Edmund's site has very long links in a single column. The links are almost verbose in the description of where they lead.

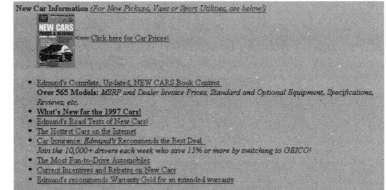

At the other extreme is the old Disney site, shown in Figure 3.2. This site uses much shorter links in a three-column format. There is little or no additional description about what the links are.

FIGURE 3.2

The old Disney site uses very short, terse links. They are arranged in three columns.

Education, fun local events: all at family.com

BOOKS
Disney Publishing

HOME VIDEO
Aladdin and the King of Thieves
Toy Story
Walt Disney Home Video

MOVIES
101 Dalmatians
The Hunchback of Notre Dame
Walt Disney Pictures

MUSIC
Walt Disney Records

Win prizes! Trips! A car! A shopping spree! More!

SHOPPING
The Disney Store Online
Send a Pooh Gram

SOFTWARE
Disney Interactive
Disney's Toy Story
Walt Disney World Explorer
Bill Nye the Science Guy

TELEVISION
The Disney Channel
Walt Disney Television

Find that special valentine at The Disney Store Online!

THEATER
Beauty & the Beast

THEME PARKS / VACATIONS
Disneyland
Walt Disney World
Disney Institute

THE WALT DISNEY COMPANY
Investor Information

INTERNATIONAL SITES

Descriptiveness Aids Prediction

Links on the Edmund's site worked well. Most of the Edmund's links explicitly describe the *content* of the page they lead to (e.g., "How to Read the Pricing and Rating Listings"). If the link itself doesn't contain this information, it's often followed by a short descriptive blurb. As one user said, "I know what I'm going to get." Users could confidently predict where the link would lead.

Link descriptions also helped users on the Fidelity site. The links shown in Figure 3.3 are actually GIF images, and the descriptions are just plain text. As this page loaded, the descriptions appeared first. Users sometimes made their decision and clicked on the text (which wasn't a link) before the GIF links even appeared, so clearly the additional information helped them decide.

FIGURE 3.3

On the Fidelity site, users sometimes made their decisions based on the text description before the GIF link image finished loading.

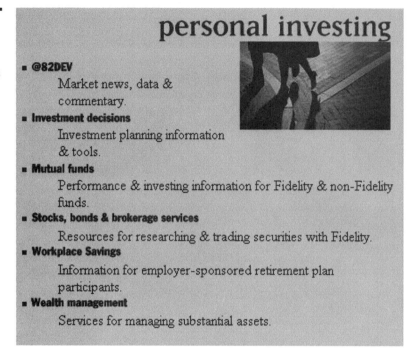

In contrast, most of the Disney links provide little information about the content of the page they lead to. If you click on Disneyland, does this bring up a map of the park? Ticket information? Special tour packages? All of the above? The "Disneyland" link text isn't so much a description of the content as an organization of it. The user must guess where this link leads. (The link actually goes to a Disneyland subsite containing all of the above information and more.)

We saw a similar problem with the C|net site. Some of its links (such as Product finder, BUYDIRECT.COM, and SOFTWARE.COM) do not differentiate their content well.

Many users picked the wrong one the first time, and several users picked wrong links more than once.

When people are searching for information, they pick links based on their expectation of the page the link will take them to. In the Inc. site, we asked users to find the phone number of the local Chamber of Commerce. Look at the screen in Figure 3.4. Which link would you choose?

BEYOND THE MAGAZINE

Articles and interviews available only online: *Inc.* Real Time, Zinc, Online Entrepreneur, and Between the Pages.

VIRTUAL CONSULTANT

Try out our interactive worksheets and searchable databases. Visit the reference desk, software libraries, bulletin boards, and Web links. Create your own Web site.

INC. MAGAZINE

Read the current issue and *Inc.*'s archives (over 5,000 articles). Information about *Inc.*, Inc. Online, and subscriptions. The *Inc.* 500 area.

INC. BUSINESS RESOURCES

Inc. products, conferences, and consulting services. The Positive Performer customer service awards. Inc. World Boston and San Diego expos.

FIGURE 3.4

In the Inc. site, we asked users to find the phone number of the local Chamber of Commerce. Most users looked in *Inc.* BUSINESS RESOURCES, but the answer was in databases.

About 90% of the time, our users picked the *Inc.* BUSINESS RESOURCES link, because it most closely matches the content they're looking for. The answer is actually found under <u>databases</u>. "Databases" is just a catchall term; the link by itself doesn't adequately describe the content.

Consider also the Travelocity Registration screen shown in Figure 3.5. Users who had never visited the site before didn't know what to do. The <u>Be Our Guest</u> link takes users to a screen where they can create a login name and password. But the "Be Our Guest" wording doesn't adequately describe the content.

Be Our Guest

You'll have full access to travel reservations and information but without the added value of a preference profile. <u>Create</u> a simple Login Name and Password, then be on your way!

Note that the terse <u>Create</u> link embedded in the paragraph didn't work very well either; more on embedded links later.

Ambiguous Terms in Links

Sometimes, terms that have a specific meaning to the interface designer may not have that same meaning for users. This isn't just an issue for web pages; it crops up in virtually all software interfaces. In our testing, we saw a few instances when ambiguous terminology in links led users seriously astray.

On the Disney site, users tended to confuse Disneyland with Disney World — they knew they were different places, but they couldn't remember which one was in Florida. While searching for information about Disney World (the one in Florida), half the users followed the wrong link and literally got "lost in Disneyland!" There is nothing in the interface that helps users differentiate between these similar names, and the Disneyland home page has no links to Disney World.

On the Fidelity site, we saw a problem with the terms "Global" and "International." We asked users to research the risk of international investment opportunities, and several people clicked the Global Network link, which provides access to other Fidelity sites around the world. One user ended up looking at a prospectus written in German. Another found herself at the Fidelity Hong Kong site, where she did her best to answer the question by looking at currency exchange rates.

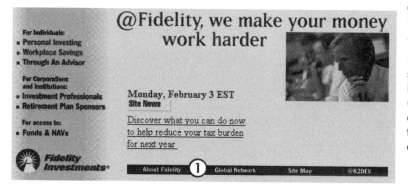

FIGURE 3.6

The link to Global Network ① led some users astray because they didn't understand the distinction between the terms "Global" and "International."

The most striking thing about these problems was that *none of these users ever realized they were in the wrong place!* They knew they hadn't found the right answer, but they couldn't explain where they had gone wrong.

Problems like these are hard for designers to predict, because they often have a different understanding of site terminology than users do. And because users themselves may not realize there's a problem, the only way to discover these problems is by directly observing users.

Dealing with Ambiguity

The Edmund's site has a different strategy for dealing with some of its ambiguous terms. The site is extensively cross-linked, so even if users aren't in the right place, they can get there. For example, the New Cars page contains a link to new trucks and sport utility vehicles, in case users go to the New Cars page mistakenly.

Fidelity tried to address the ambiguous terms problem by having a dictionary of terms used on the site. However, the dictionary page took so long to load that one of the two users who tried to use it simply gave up. The other user never found the definition she needed.

"Differentness" Aids Navigation

If users couldn't predict which link would get them to the content they sought, they'd try to eliminate links that seem obviously wrong and pick the one that is left.

Some sites had similar links that made it harder for the user to do this. For example, the Travelocity site has three similar-sounding links: 3 Best Itineraries, Flights & Prices, and Fares, as shown in Figure 3.7. Which one would you select to find the best available round-trip airfare from Boston to London? (The correct answer is 3 Best Itineraries.)

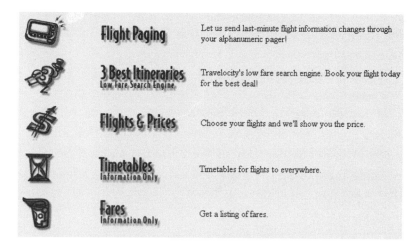

FIGURE 3.7

Travelocity has three similar-sounding choices for finding flights.

The WebSaver site had similarly indistinguishable links. For example, should a user trying to learn about annuities pick <u>Select the WebSaver Annuity that's right for you</u> or <u>Is the WebSaver Annuity Right For Me</u>? Each link leads to a different page.

The Hewlett Packard site shown in Figure 3.8 finished near the top of our rankings. Interestingly, users chose the correct link on the first try. Perhaps this can be attributed at least partially to how different the links are from each other.

FIGURE 3.8

Users generally started with the correct link on the Hewlett Packard site, perhaps because the links are well differentiated.

Number of Links

Our analysis found a negative correlation between number of links and success. In general, the more links on a page that led to other pages, the harder it was for users to answer our test questions.

We aren't sure how to interpret this. But imagine an artificially simple page that only has two links: the user would have a 50/50 chance of guessing the right path. The odds of guessing correctly decrease as more links are added. So it's possible that having too many links may interfere with the user's process of elimination.

But this doesn't necessarily imply that fewer links are better. The Edmund's home page has redundant links — there are three ways to get to the New Cars page, as seen in Figure 3.9. Different users chose different ones to get to the information. Redundant links seemed to work for Edmund's.

FIGURE 3.9

Edmund's has redundant links: two text links ①② and one image ③ that all lead to the New Cars page.

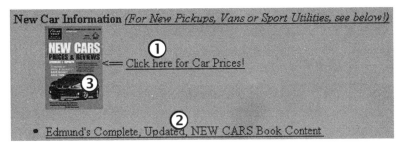

Image Links

A weak positive correlation exists between image links (such as graphics that look like buttons) and user success. However, we saw one minor problem with image links: because they don't change color after the user clicks them, there is no visual cue that they have already been traversed. Users did use visual cues to initially identify the image links by moving the mouse across the page and watching for the cursor to change to Netscape Navigator's pointing finger.

The lack of visual cues can interfere with the user's process of elimination in deciding what link to choose. Consider what we saw in testing the Fidelity site: After eliminating the other links on the home page, users clicked the @82DEV button, as shown in Figure 3.10. This link led to one of Fidelity's sister sites.

FIGURE 3.10

Because image links don't change color, some users chose the @82DEV link several times, even though it was not what they wanted.

After discovering they'd gone down a rat hole, users returned to Fidelity's home page, looked at all the links and eliminated those they thought weren't applicable... and then clicked the @82DEV button again. Some users repeated this process more than once.

Link Layout

All links were not created equal. We found some differences in user success based on how the links are laid out on the web page.

Embedded Links

Putting text around links doesn't seem to work well. We found a strong negative correlation between embedded links (those surrounded by text) and user success in finding information.

FIGURE 3.11

Examples of embedded and non-embedded links. The embedded links seem to impair a user's performance.

This _embedded link_ is surrounded by text

We called this an embedded link since it is followed by text

We did not call this an embedded link
The additional descriptive text appears on a separate line

Some pages use a terse link embedded within a sentence or paragraph, such as the Create link on Travelocity's registration screen (see Figure 3.5). The Inc. site (Figure 3.4) also uses a lot of embedded links.

When links are contained within other text, it is harder for users to pick the link they want. We believe this is because users skim rather than read. When users are searching for something specific, they scan a page looking for relevant links. If they must stop, back up, and read the surrounding material to understand the context, they will go more slowly.

On the other hand, if the link itself contains or is followed by a description of its content, users can more readily eliminate those links that don't apply. They only have to look more closely at those they haven't eliminated.

Wrapped Links

Anything that causes a link to wrap across multiple lines can damage its effectiveness. Users didn't always realize that a link wrapped across two or more lines was actually a single link. Wrapped links are more likely to occur with longer links or multiple-column formats.

Wrapped links on the Fidelity site caused one user to answer one of our questions incorrectly. We had asked how many money market funds Fidelity offers. Figure 3.12 shows how the list of three mutual funds appears to the user.

FIGURE 3.12

Fidelity's wrapped links caused one user to conclude that Fidelity offers five mutual funds, not just three.

This user perceived the "Federal Municipal Money Market" wrapped link as two separate links, as evidenced by his behavior. He first clicked the "Federal Municipal" part and read the text that appeared in the frame. He then clicked the "Money Market" part (nothing on the screen changed, because he was already there) and read the text — the same text — again. He went back and forth at least half a dozen times, trying to determine if anything was different. When we asked him, he couldn't explain why "the links didn't seem to work." He did not look at the URL information in Netscape Navigator's status line. He finally concluded that Fidelity has five mutual funds.

Edmund's clarified wrapped links by adding bullets, but one trade-off with this approach is that it requires additional space for the bullet and indenting.

Link Destinations

We saw some interesting issues with links that take users to another place on the same page (within-page links) and links that take users to other sites. Our observations imply that users may have a mental model that links will take them to another page within the same site.

Within-Page Links

Overall, within-page links (which take the user to another location in the same page) showed a slight positive correlation with success at finding information. However, these links sometimes cause confusion.

We saw this particularly in the Edmund's site, which had a very long home page and several within-page links at the top. Some users began by scrolling down the page, then scrolled back to the top and clicked the <u>New Cars</u> link. This link took them partway down the page, where they scanned the information and often went past it into the next section. Then they went back to the top and clicked the next within-page link, which took them to the part of the page they had just left. Some users repeated this process more than once until they realized it took them to the same place they'd already been. Others used these links without difficulty.

It's possible to avoid within-page links by making each page short. Fidelity's pages were short (as described in Chapter 6, Readability and Page Layout) but we didn't find any evidence that they worked any better than longer pages. Our findings suggest that within-page links did more good than harm in helping users find information.

Links to Other Sites

Users did not realize that some links took them to other sites. While searching several sites (most notably C|net), users went off to other sites for several minutes and were totally unaware that they had left the original site. They were puzzled by the disappearance of the link structure and appearance of the initial site and by their inability to get back to the home page (many users did not use the Back button in the browser). Users who ended up at another site but did not realize it found themselves in a perplexing situation.

For example, in the C|net test we asked users to find which of the top three recommended digital cameras is the least expensive. The results of the C|net Product Finder (a search tool) had links to several manufacturers' sites, as shown in Figure 3.13.

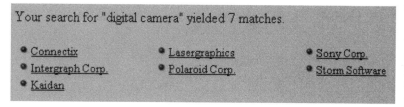

Your search for "digital camera" yielded 7 matches.

- Connectix
- Intergraph Corp.
- Kaidan
- Lasergraphics
- Polaroid Corp.
- Sony Corp.
- Storm Software

These links led to C|net's reviews of these manufacturers' sites. Within the reviews, there were links to the sites themselves. Users didn't realize that the links in the reviews caused them to leave the C|net and go to a different site. One user looked through the Polaroid site for pricing information (which Polaroid does not provide) and then gave up, concluding that it was C|net that didn't have this information (which it did, elsewhere).

FIGURE 3.13

These links in C|net's Product Finder lead to C|net's reviews of these sites, but links within the reviews go to the actual manufacturers' sites. Users didn't realize when links went off-site, and one user blamed C|net for a lack of information at the Polaroid site.

Will Experience Help?

What about users who return to a site frequently? Over time, as they become familiar with the content, will they learn to make accurate predictions based on terse, lower-content links?

Since we studied only first-time use of these sites rather than repeated use, we don't know how true this may be. All we can say is that we saw very little evidence of learning *during* our tests — once users got stuck on something, it kept giving them trouble.

When it comes to learning through experience, the hurdles for web sites may be even higher than they are for conventional software due to the sheer number of sites. If a user has visited a site 50 times, but has visited 200 other sites in the same time span, is that user experienced? Does that exposure to other sites help or hurt? We don't know.

Within-Site Searching

We didn't tell users to use the site's search mechanism to find answers, but many of them did. About one-third of the people we tested usually tried a search as their initial strategy, and others resorted to it when they couldn't find an answer by following links.

Most of the sites we studied had built-in search engines to help users find information within the site. Edmund's, WebSaver, and Travelocity did not, and one user gave up on a task in Edmund's when he couldn't find a search facility.

Sometimes the search engine helped, but often it didn't. Users had two types of problems with on-site searches:

- They didn't understand the scope of the search.
- They had trouble interpreting the search results.

Unclear Search Areas

Users were often confused about what parts of a site the search engine would examine. They tended to assume that a search would cover the entire site and didn't always realize when it would search in just one particular area. Or, if there were obviously several different ways to search, users didn't know which one to try first.

Multiple Areas

The Disney search engine covers all areas of the site, but this fact is initially hidden from the user. The site is huge, containing more than 7,000 pages. Searching the entire Disney site to find the cheapest hotel on the Walt Disney World monorail is like using an atlas to find your way out of the woods. Users went to Disney's Find page, and entered "Walt Disney World Monorail" for the search, as shown in Figure 4.1. Notice that there's no indication of which parts of the site will be included in the search.

FIGURE 4.1

When the user starts a search, the Disney site does not indicate all of the areas that are included in the search.

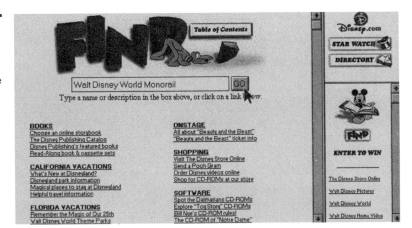

At the end of the search results, users are presented with another search field. Unlike the original search, users now have the opportunity to specify only certain areas, as shown in Figure 4.2. But to reach this point, the user has to wade through a long list of results, many of which are not relevant.

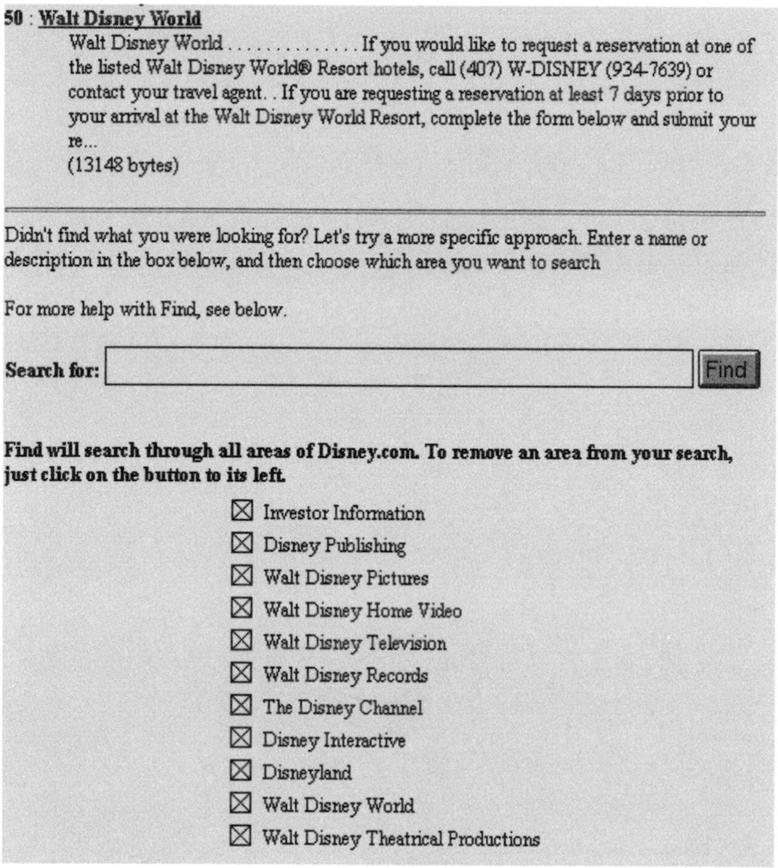

50 : **Walt Disney World**

Walt Disney World . . . . If you would like to request a reservation at one of the listed Walt Disney World® Resort hotels, call (407) W-DISNEY (934-7639) or contact your travel agent. . If you are requesting a reservation at least 7 days prior to your arrival at the Walt Disney World Resort, complete the form below and submit your re...
(13148 bytes)

Didn't find what you were looking for? Let's try a more specific approach. Enter a name or description in the box below, and then choose which area you want to search

For more help with Find, see below.

Search for: [   ] [Find]

Find will search through all areas of Disney.com. To remove an area from your search, just click on the button to its left.

☒ Investor Information
☒ Disney Publishing
☒ Walt Disney Pictures
☒ Walt Disney Home Video
☒ Walt Disney Television
☒ Walt Disney Records
☒ The Disney Channel
☒ Disney Interactive
☒ Disneyland
☒ Walt Disney World
☒ Walt Disney Theatrical Productions

FIGURE 4.2

Only after displaying the initial results does the Disney search give the user the option to specify which areas to exclude.

Search "Tar Pits"

When people got really lost, they often went to the nearest search engine to get themselves pointed in the right direction. But when the user is deep within the site, some search engines only search the narrow set of topics related to the user's current location. Because the search looked only at the section of the site users were currently in, the search didn't help them get out of the "tar pit" they were stuck in.

The C|net site works this way. When users were lost in Product Finder, doing a search never got them out to related information in other parts of the site. This caused some users to give up.

Confusing Search Areas

The Fidelity site attempted to clarify the scope of searches by labeling the different search areas. As Figure 4.3 shows, users had to select a portion of the site to search. But most users weren't able to determine whether they should search Fidelity Mutual Funds, Fidelity Daily NAVs, or Personal Investing because they didn't know the differences among these three areas. Typing the same keyword into each category produced completely different results, and this surprised the users.

FIGURE 4.3

In Fidelity's search, users didn't understand the search areas and had trouble deciding which one to choose.

Search allows you to find all documents on our site containing the word or phrase entered in the field below. You can use parentheses, booleans (**AND, OR,** and **NOT**), and wildcards.

For example you could select Fidelity Mutual Funds, enter Microsoft in the Keywords field, and hit Begin Search. The site would then return a list of all Mutual Funds that have as one of its top ten holdings as of a certain date Microsoft.

Choose Search Area: Fidelity Mutual Funds
Fidelity Mutual Funds
Fidelity Daily NAVs
Enter Keyword(s): Personal Investing

Maximum Documents to Return: 25

Begin Search   Reset Search

Inc.'s "Searchable Databases" covers multiple areas, as shown in Figure 4.4. Even for a task as simple as looking up the phone number of the local chamber of commerce, users didn't know which search engine they should use, or whether they could use more than one at a time.

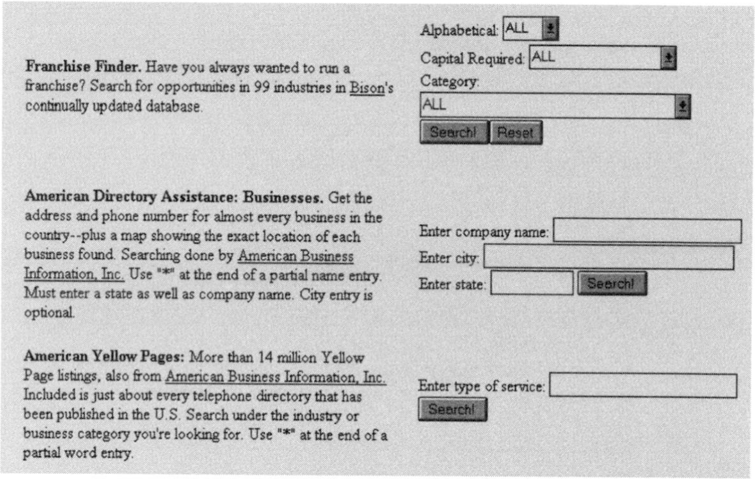

FIGURE 4.4

This excerpt from Inc.'s search shows just three of the dozen search areas the user must choose from.

Fidelity and Inc. are just two examples — we also saw search area problems on other sites. This issue complicates the user's task, because in addition to deciding what keywords to type in, the user must also decide *where* to start looking.

Search Results

Correctly specifying the search area was only half the battle. Users often had trouble interpreting and using the search results.

Organization of Search Results

All of the search engines we tested presented results as a (seemingly) unsorted list of items. For some sites, like Disney, the resulting list contained page titles and the first 30 or so words on the page, as shown in Figure 4.5.

None of the lists were organized in a way that users understood. The search engines may have been using a relevance algorithm, but it often wasn't clear to users why a particular item was returned.

FIGURE 4.5

When users searched for "Walt Disney World monorail" they had a hard time interpreting the results. Even with the accompanying blurb, they couldn't tell which items were relevant to their task.

45 : **Walt Disney World**
Walt Disney World . . JANUARY THROUGH DECEMBER 1997 .(Rates are per person, based on adult double occupancy.) . .BASIC PLAN .Includes accommodations, Disney Institute programs and evening entertainment, One-Day/One-Park Ticket to any Walt Disney World
(9757 bytes)

46 : **Walt Disney World's Frequently Asked Questions**
Walt Disney World's Frequently Asked Questions . . . . Frequently Asked Questions about the Walt Disney World
(10112 bytes)

47 : **Walt Disney World**
Walt Disney World . . . . .Choosing a Package makes vacation planning a breeze. They're worry-free, so you can devote all your time to enjoying the fun. Vacation packages feature Disney Resort hotels and give you exclusive benefits and privileges. Disney Institute Vacation Packages .Disney's Summer Magic Package . The best way to experienc...
(8511 bytes)

48 : **Walt Disney World**
Walt Disney World . . . . .Map Out Your Walt Disney World Fun! . Interactive maps make it easy for you to find your way around our 46-square-mile Vacation Kingdom. You can tour the Parks by clicking on different map locations and checking QuickTime VR for a 360-degree look around the Parks. Interactive Maps - NEW maps for 1997!.(Updated 1...
(11058 bytes)

49 : **Walt Disney World**
Walt Disney World . . . . .Features. | .Hours. | .Restaurants. | .Location/Transportation. | .Tickets .As legend has it, Blizzard Beach was created by a freak winter storm that dropped snow over the western side of Walt Disney World property. Temperatures soared, however, and as water began to cascade down Mt. Gushmore, the first sk...
(11296 bytes)

Scanning lists of search results was more difficult than we expected. One user repeatedly grumbled, "I don't like to read lists." Another failed in searches because he chose a plausible (but incorrect) item too soon, before the obviously correct one appeared further down in the list.

Not Enough Information

Frequently, the information returned by the search engine was not enough to help users know whether they wanted to follow a link or not. Many search engines (such as those on Hewlett Packard and Fidelity) return web page titles, which are rarely descriptive of their content.

For example, when users searched for "international investments" on the Fidelity site, they received the list of filenames shown in Figure 4.6.

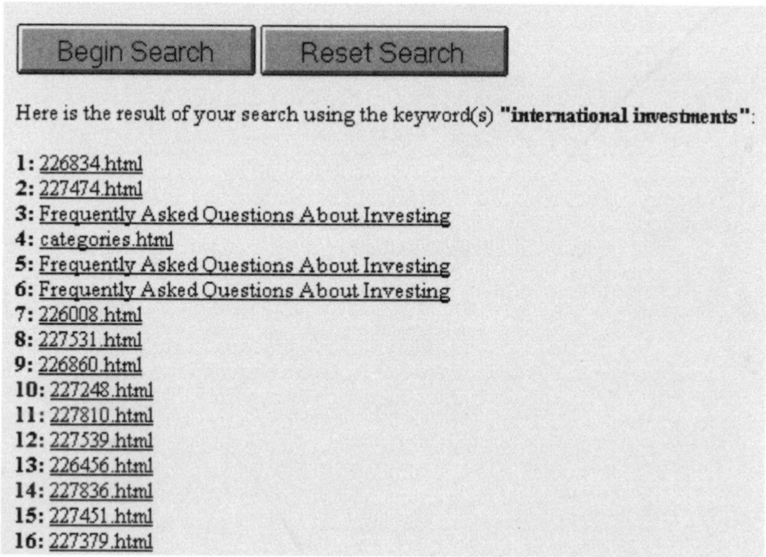

Here is the result of your search using the keyword(s) **"international investments"**:

1: 226834.html
2: 227474.html
3: Frequently Asked Questions About Investing
4: categories.html
5: Frequently Asked Questions About Investing
6: Frequently Asked Questions About Investing
7: 226008.html
8: 227531.html
9: 226860.html
10: 227248.html
11: 227810.html
12: 227539.html
13: 226456.html
14: 227836.html
15: 227451.html
16: 227379.html

FIGURE 4.6

If you search for "international investments" on the Fidelity site, you receive a list of filenames. Users didn't find this helpful.

Compare this with the same site's "frequently asked questions about international investments," shown in Figure 4.7. The FAQ topics are definitely more helpful to users than the search results.

FIGURE 4.7

Fidelity's FAQ for "international investments" is both shorter and more descriptive than the search results.

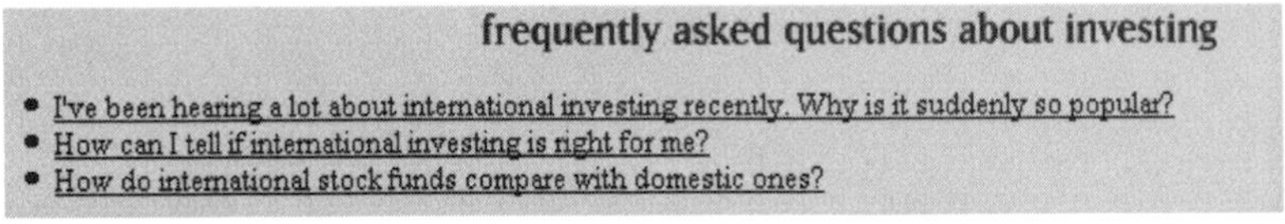

frequently asked questions about investing

- I've been hearing a lot about international investing recently. Why is it suddenly so popular?
- How can I tell if international investing is right for me?
- How do international stock funds compare with domestic ones?

Redundant Information

Users didn't like it when the search engine returned multiple instances of the same link. For example, Figure 4.8 shows what you get on the Hewlett Packard site if you search for "laserjet 4v." Many of the links are the same. And when a user follows one of them, only that link changes color even though others lead to the same page.

FIGURE 4.8

Many of Hewlett Packard's search results are redundant, and include links to non-English pages.

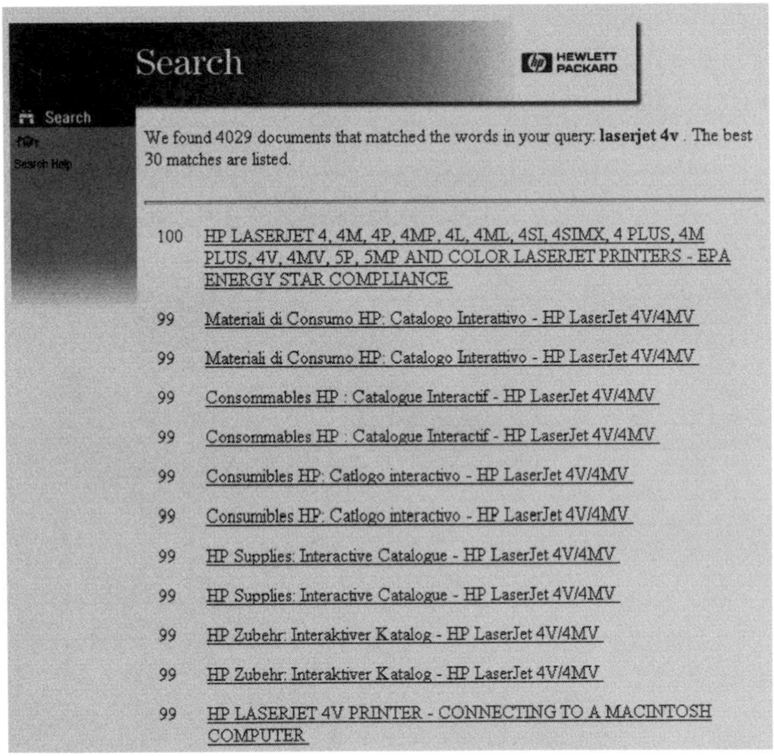

Search   *hp* HEWLETT PACKARD

Search
tor
Search Help

We found 4029 documents that matched the words in your query: **laserjet 4v** . The best 30 matches are listed.

100   HP LASERJET 4, 4M, 4P, 4MP, 4L, 4ML, 4SI, 4SIMX, 4 PLUS, 4M PLUS, 4V, 4MV, 5P, 5MP AND COLOR LASERJET PRINTERS - EPA ENERGY STAR COMPLIANCE

99   Materiali di Consumo HP: Catalogo Interattivo - HP LaserJet 4V/4MV

99   Materiali di Consumo HP: Catalogo Interattivo - HP LaserJet 4V/4MV

99   Consommables HP : Catalogue Interactif - HP LaserJet 4V/4MV

99   Consommables HP : Catalogue Interactif - HP LaserJet 4V/4MV

99   Consumibles HP: Catlogo interactivo - HP LaserJet 4V/4MV

99   Consumibles HP: Catlogo interactivo - HP LaserJet 4V/4MV

99   HP Supplies: Interactive Catalogue - HP LaserJet 4V/4MV

99   HP Supplies: Interactive Catalogue - HP LaserJet 4V/4MV

99   HP Zubehr: Interaktiver Katalog - HP LaserJet 4V/4MV

99   HP Zubehr: Interaktiver Katalog - HP LaserJet 4V/4MV

99   HP LASERJET 4V PRINTER - CONNECTING TO A MACINTOSH COMPUTER

Useless Information

Perhaps not everything should be included in a search! For example, when one user searched the Personal Investing section of the Fidelity site for "international," the first four items listed were "INTERNATIONAL DATA - AD." When users clicked on the first item, the pictures shown in Figure 4.9 appeared on the screen one after the other about five seconds apart.

FIGURE 4.9

These Fidelity ad images showed up in a search. They were completely out of context, and users were annoyed and frustrated by them.

These images come from an advertisement that ran in a frame on the Fidelity site. They appeared in the search results because their text closely matched the user's search string, "international." The Fidelity search picked up advertising in addition to actual site content. (We don't know whether this was deliberate.) Apparently, the relevance algorithm used by the search engine boosted these ads to the top of the results list. But users got frustrated by what they called the "garbage" returned by the search, and they stopped using it.

CHAPTER 5

The Difficulty of Comparisons

Making comparisons is tougher than we thought! Since most web sites try, at least indirectly, to sell products, we expected the sites to help users make decisions. But after watching users try to answer comparative questions, it seems that most sites are not designed to help people compare information.

We asked users to answer comparison questions at each site. These required them to find information in two or more places. For example, we asked users to find the best convertible for under $20,000. They had to research all the models.

Users found these questions much harder than the non-comparison questions. We weren't surprised by this — after all, comparison questions require at least twice as much work. We were surprised, however, by the significance of the difference. After each question, users rated their energy level. The highest energy level reported after a comparison question was lower than the lowest energy level they reported after a non-comparison question.

How Users Handled Comparisons

Users clearly struggled with comparisons. This was most evident in the strategies they used.

Remembering

Some users would try to rely on their memories to help them compare information. They'd find one option, try to remember the salient points, then find another option. We saw a lot of flipping back and forth between the options, and a lot of inaccurate answers. Not surprisingly, human memory proved to be quite fallible.

Writing Things Down

Repeatedly, we saw users write down one piece of information and then go to another page and look at something else. This was particularly true when people were comparing numbers. For example, when we asked whether the Chinese men's or the US women's swim team completed the Olympic 400-meter medley relay fastest, users tended to write down the first answer they found.

Printing

We also saw users print various pages. For example, when we asked users to find the best convertible for under $20,000, one user printed out the descriptions of all the cars that fit the description (there were three), placed them side by side on the floor, and made the decision that way.

Interestingly, about half the time, users made their decisions before retrieving the pages from the printer.

Opening Multiple Windows

We also saw users try to compare two pieces of information side by side on the screen. No site supported this, but one user opened two browser windows to look at several pieces of information simultaneously.

Multiple Comparisons and "Pogo-Sticking"

When users needed to compare several different items — more than three or four — they expressed frustration. We refer to this as a "pogo-stick" problem because users have to hop up and down to get to the information they need. This happens most often when the site's hierarchy is based on a list of options, usually only in text form. Users jump down to one option, read it, go back up to the list, choose another, jump down, and so on.

The new Disney site shows this. We asked users to figure out which CD they'd like to buy for their niece. All of the choices were listed on one page as shown in Figure 5.1, and users had to navigate up and down repeatedly to get the detailed descriptions for all their options. This even caused one user to give up, saying "Forget this. I'll just order the catalog."

FIGURE 5.1

When we asked users to figure out which CD they'd buy, they had to navigate up and down repeatedly to get the detailed descriptions for all the options.

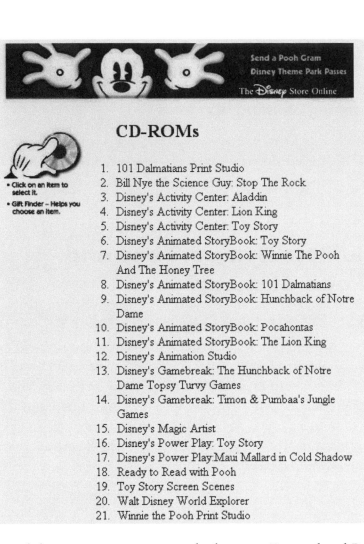

We did see users trying to use the browser Forward and Back buttons to help with comparisons, but that strategy didn't work well either. The Back button took them back to the list of options, and the Forward button took them to the page they had already seen.

Designs That Prevent Pogo-Sticking

The Travelocity site created lists of options, requiring users to drill down to see each item. Travelocity, however, included Previous and Next buttons to let users move sideways within the list, as shown in Figure 5.2. We thought this would be an effective strategy, and several users did use these buttons.

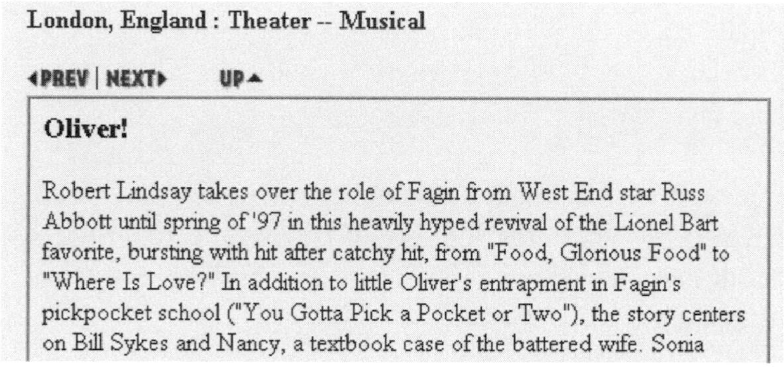

London, England : Theater -- Musical

◄PREV | NEXT►   UP▲

Oliver!

Robert Lindsay takes over the role of Fagin from West End star Russ Abbott until spring of '97 in this heavily hyped revival of the Lionel Bart favorite, bursting with hit after catchy hit, from "Food, Glorious Food" to "Where Is Love?" In addition to little Oliver's entrapment in Fagin's pickpocket school ("You Gotta Pick a Pocket or Two"), the story centers on Bill Sykes and Nancy, a textbook case of the battered wife. Sonia

FIGURE 5.2

The Travelocity site tried to minimize pogo-sticking with its Previous, Next, and Up buttons.

Similarly, when users went to the car model descriptions on the Edmund's site, each page had links to similar models, as shown in Figure 5.3. We thought these links might be useful but no one used them, even though we gave users two comparison questions on the site.

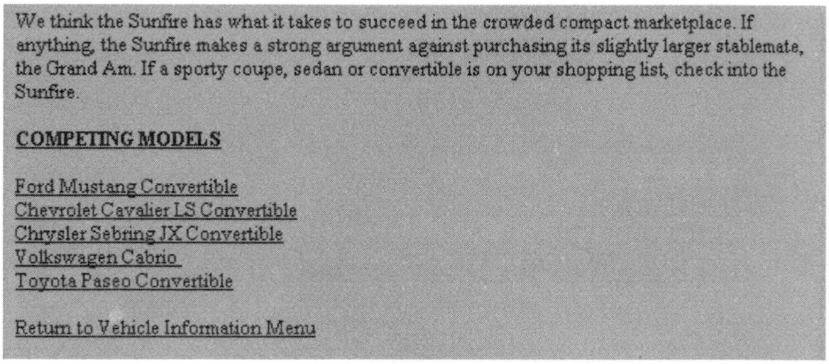

We think the Sunfire has what it takes to succeed in the crowded compact marketplace. If anything, the Sunfire makes a strong argument against purchasing its slightly larger stablemate, the Grand Am. If a sporty coupe, sedan or convertible is on your shopping list, check into the Sunfire.

COMPETING MODELS

Ford Mustang Convertible
Chevrolet Cavalier LS Convertible
Chrysler Sebring JX Convertible
Volkswagen Cabrio
Toyota Paseo Convertible

Return to Vehicle Information Menu

FIGURE 5.3

The Edmund's site had links to comparable models of cars. We thought this might help, but no one we tested used these links.

The Catalog Approach

The Olympic site used more of a catalog approach, which seemed to frustrate users less. We asked users if there was any Olympic clothing they'd be interested in buying.

The merchandise page of the Olympic site contained thumbnail pictures and brief descriptions of all the clothing, much like a mail-order catalog. Users got enough of an idea about each item to decide whether it was worth investigating further. If it was, they'd drill down and get a larger picture and more detailed description.

This approach is also a pogo-stick construction, but there is enough content in the top-level list of options to let users easily eliminate those choices that are obviously not what they want.

Sites That Help You Choose

Most of the sites we studied did little to support comparisons. A few, however, attempted to help users choose between options by asking the user to complete a short questionnaire.

The Travelocity site seemed to do the best job. To select a flight, users could enter their destination, preferred departure date and time, and so on. The system would present them with three itineraries — or lists of flights — that met their criteria, as shown in Figure 5.4.

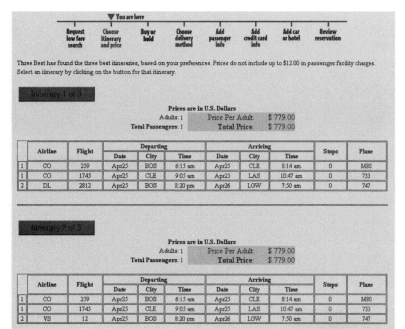

FIGURE 5.4

Travelocity presented users with a list of three itineraries that met their criteria.

On the WebSaver site, users could fill out a form to help them determine which of four annuities best met their needs, as shown in Figure 5.5. Several users found the form and filled it out, but distrusted the results. They were skeptical that the WebSaver site would really recommend an annuity that was best for them. Instead, they thought that whatever annuity the site recommended would be the one that was most profitable for the company.

Is the WebSaver Annuity Right For Me?

The WebSaver Annuity may not be the right retirement savings choice for everyone. Answer these five questions to see if the WebSaver Annuity may be right for you

1. Are you already contributing the maximum amount you can to tax-qualified retirement plans for which you qualify - such as IRA, 401(k), 403(b), or KEOGH plans?

   ○ YES ○ NO

2. Are you concerned that your current retirement savings program may not be sufficient to provide real financial security and independence for your retirement?

   ○ YES ○ NO

3. Do you realistically have at least $2,000 you can set aside for retirement --- money that you don't expect to need for upcoming bills?

   ○ YES ○ NO

4. Do you already own an annuity?

   ○ YES ○ NO

5. WebSaver Annuity pays competitive guaranteed fixed rates that reflect the efficiency of direct World Wide Web distribution. Would you consider an attractive tax deferred fixed rate instrument for your supplemental retirement savings?

   ○ YES ○ NO

[Proceed] [Clear My Answers]

Recently, the Hewlett Packard site added a questionnaire to help users figure out which printer is best for them, as shown in Figure 5.6. The form returns a list of printers that meet the user's needs, as shown in Figure 5.7. We haven't tested this, so we don't know whether it actually helps.

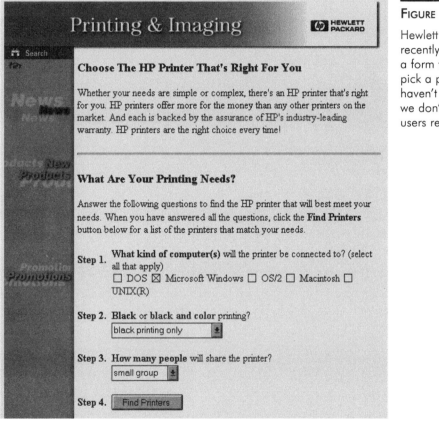

FIGURE 5.6

Hewlett Packard recently implemented a form to help users pick a printer. We haven't tested it, so we don't know how users react to it.

FIGURE 5.7

The Hewlett Packard form returns a list of printers that meet a user's needs. Although we haven't tested this with users, it does provide the type of side-by-side comparison that all our test sites lacked.

HP Printers For You

Here are the HP printers that best match your requirements:

- Microsoft Windows
- black printing only
- small group

or, you may go back and change your requirements. The printers in the table below are arranged in order from lowest price to highest.

```
                                     Black                Print Speed   Page
                          Platforms  Print     Print      (pages/min)   per
Cost   HP Printer         Supported  Quality   Tech        B/W color    Mont
-----  ------------------ ---------  -------  -------     ------ -----   -----
    $  LaserJet 6P        S S S O O  *****    Laser         8            12,0
    $  LaserJet 6MP       S S S S O  *****    Laser         8            12,0
   $$  LaserJet 5P        S S S O O  *****    Laser         6            12,0
   $$  LaserJet 5MP       S S S S O  *****    Laser         6            12,0
   $$  LaserJet 5         S S S O O  *****    Laser        12            35,
   $$  LaserJet 5N        S S S O S  *****    Laser        12            35,
  $$$  LaserJet 4V        S S S O O  *****    Laser        16            50,
 $$$$  LaserJet 4MV       S S S S S  *****    Laser        16            50,
                          | | | | |
                    DOS-+ | | | +- Unix
                    Win----+ | +-----Mac
                    OS/2------+

Legend
------
Platforms Supported:
S: Standard
O: Optional
-: Unsupported
```

CHAPTER 6

Readability and Page Layout

"If you are a designer, you'll be glad to know that the same rules of design apply to the web as to print — or any other medium."

— Ben Benjamin
http://www.cnet.com/Content/Features/Howto/Design/index.html

People have been putting text and pictures on computer screens for 30 years or more, so we didn't expect to find anything new in the area of page layout and design. Conventional wisdom and most of the popular web design books suggest an approach similar to traditional screen design or paper.

It's not that easy, however. We were surprised to see that some "old standards" of page layout, like white-space and horizontal rules, have their drawbacks on web sites. And we were dumbfounded when we saw the statistics about how text readability affects user success and perceptions.

Our Theory: Skimming Is In

The results in this chapter are easier to understand when you consider that most of the people we tested didn't read all the information on a page. They scanned the text as they searched for an answer. Only when they found something that looked plausible did they actually read the text. Page layouts that made skimming easy fared better than those that didn't.

Readability and the Web

Readability measures like the Gunning Fog Index and Flesch-Kincaid Grade Level scale were developed to calculate how "readable" a passage of text is. These scales attempt to measure reading difficulty by words, sentences, syllables, and so on, then feeding those numbers into an algorithm.

We had theorized that the easier a page was to read (according to these measures), the more usable it would be. In fact, however, we found exactly the opposite:

- The less readable a site was, the more users were successful with the site.
- The less readable a site was, the more users found the site:
    - authoritative,
    - clear,
    - complete,
    - satisfying, and
    - useful.

- The less readable a site was, the less likely users found the site:
  - overwhelming and
  - over-detailed.

We calculated the readability of our test sites using three indices: the Gunning Fog Index, the Flesch Reading Ease, and the Flesch-Kincaid Grade Level. These tools calculate readability in different ways, as described in Table 6.1.

Index	What It Measures
Gunning Fog	The average number of words, sentences, and big words (more than three syllables). The ideal Fog index is 7 or 8. A level above 12 means that most people will not understand the document.
Flesch Reading Ease	The average number of syllables per word and words per sentence. Scores range from 0 to 100. The higher the score, the easier it is to understand the document.
Flesch-Kincaid Grade Level	The average number of syllables per word and words per sentence. The score indicates a grade level required to read the text. For example, a score of 7.0 means that a seventh-grader would understand the document.

TABLE 6.1

These three formulas calculate readability in different ways.

The Gunning Fog Index provided the highest correlation with success — the higher the Gunning Fog Index, the more successful the site. For example, Figure 6.1 shows the most readable text we tested, the new Disney site. It has a Fog Index score of 6.5. The Hewlett Packard site was the least readable, with a Fog Index of 15.3, as shown in Figure 6.2.

Calculating the Fog Index

While some word-processing tools calculate the Fog Index automatically, others do not. Here's the eight-step formula to calculate it yourself.

1. Choose a sample of text that contains at least 100 words.

2. Count the number of words in the sample.

3. Count the number of sentences.

Weekend edition   April 11-13, 1997

Pooh Makes Reading Fun!   Now on CD-ROM!

Today's Features:

Bring Pooh to life on your screen! Three new CD-ROMs let you learn, print, and play with everybody's favorite bear. You can also watch a snippet of Winnie on video — or sample a Sing-Along online.

NEW FROM DISNEY! Reserve your Charter Subscription today!

Education, fun, local events: all at family.com.

Say thank you with Pooh — order now!

STAR WATCH Click your favorite star above or see all the stars.

PLEASE CLICK HERE FOR LEGAL RESTRICTIONS AND TERMS OF USE APPLICABLE TO THIS SITE. USE OF THIS SITE SIGNIFIES YOUR AGREEMENT TO THE TERMS OF USE.

Disney. All rights reserved.

Welcome to HP Search About HP HP Financials
Jobs at HP HP Worldwide Press Releases Feature article

- Printing & Imaging

- Personal Computing

- Test & Measurement

- Electronic Components

- Industry Solutions

- Business & Technical Computing

- Networking

- Healthcare

- Chemical Analysis

- Services & Support

Ever thought of simplifying enterprise computing? We did.

Also...

- Ever thought of simplifying enterprise computing?
  We did.

- HP and Microsoft Announce Joint Strategy to
  Simplify Enterprise Computing with Integrated
  Products and Services

- HP's 1996 annual report is now available online!

[Printing & Imaging] [Personal Computing] [Test &
Measurement] [Electronic Components] [Industry
Solutions] [Business & Technical Computing] [Network-
ing] [Healthcare] [Chemical Analysis] [Services & Sup-
port]

[Search] [About HP] [Jobs at HP] [HP Worldwide] [Press
Releases] [Support Documentation and Software (Driv-
ers) for HP's PCs, Printers and Imaging Products]

Welcome to HP   Hewlett Packard Search   Contact HP
Copyright 1997 Hewlett-Packard Company

[Search HP] [Top] [Contact HP] [Copyright]

FIGURE 6.2

The text in the Hewlett
Packard site was the
least readable, with a
Gunning Fog Index
score of 15.3. It was
one of the easiest sites
to use.

4. Count the number of big words (three or more syllables).

5. Divide the number of sentences into the number of words.

6. Divide the number of words into the number of big words.

7. Add the result of step 5 to the result of step 6.

8. Multiply by 0.4. The result is the Fog Index. The ideal level is 7 or 8, and a result above 12 is considered too hard for most people to read.

Scanability

Clearly, making text harder to read isn't the answer here. What's interesting about these findings is that they measure something that makes it easier for users to find information. We don't know what that is yet, but we think it relates to making it easier for users to skim pages.

One of our theories relates to interference on the page. Hard-to-read sites have fewer conjunctions and standard grammatical structures. Since all the elements on a screen are competing for the user's attention, it makes sense that the extra words we normally use to complete a sentence may get in the way of the meaningful words in the text. Removing them, and thus making the text harder to read by traditional measures, may increase scanability.

The White-Space Dilemma

Standard design textbooks say that white-space is good. In fact, we ran across one web design book (we'll conceal the name to protect the innocent!) that said the following:

Users have to have plenty of it [white-space]. Like Japanese flower arrangements, the white-space defines the objects around it. When a user goes to your web site, the white-space makes him feel secure... White-space allows users to be able to tell one thing from another quickly. Don't clutter the page.

Surprisingly, however, we found no indication that white-space is beneficial on the web. In fact,

- The more white-space there was on a site, the less successful users were at finding information.
- The more white-space, the lower users rated the site in terms of:
  - finding things easily,
  - ease of reading,
  - ease of searching,
  - overall appearance,
  - ease of use, and
  - productivity.

White-Space and Text Density

These findings amazed us so much that we went back and found different ways to measure white-space. (Since our findings were so contrary to conventional wisdom, we assumed we must have calculated something incorrectly!)

One of the ways we measured was to print out each site's home page, then black out all the text and graphics. We then had a dozen people rank the sites from most white-space to least. Figure 6.3 shows the sites that finished at the top and bottom of the pack.

FIGURE 6.3

One way we measured white-space was by blacking out all text and graphics. The Olympic site (left) was the most dense, while the Edmund's site (right) has the most white-space.

We also calculated the density of the text using the following formula:

$$\frac{\textit{Total \# of words on page}}{\textit{Length of printed page in inches}} = \textit{Text Density}$$

Text density is easy to measure. It also correlates well (negatively) with white-space.

White-Space and Skimming

We aren't sure exactly why sites with only a little white-space do better than sites with a lot, but we have a few theories. Skimming is, by definition, a very different activity than reading. When people are hunting for information, they benefit by covering a lot of ground quickly. White-space spreads out the information and slows the hunt.

Also, looking at text on a web page is different from looking at text in a newspaper, for example. In a newspaper, the reader can see the whole page at once. This is not true for web sites, which are viewed through the window of a browser. The reader is forced to construct the page in his or her head.

Scrolling and "the Fold"

Conventional wisdom dictates that users don't like to scroll, hence all information on a page should be "above the fold." This is newspaper terminology that defines where on the page the most important stuff goes. For example, a story that is "page 1, above the fold" is considered very important news.

In web page design, the fold signifies the place at which the user has to scroll down to get more information. Since users have screens with different resolutions and run their browsers at different window sizes, the placement of the fold is difficult for the designer to control.

The Fidelity site, more than any other site we tested, went to great lengths to have many of its pages completely above the fold, as shown in Figure 6.4. The result is lots of pages, each with small amounts of content. There was no evidence to suggest that this strategy either helped or hurt.

In fact, we never saw any user frustration with scrolling. For instance, when we counted "first clicks" — the first place people clicked when they came to a new site — clicks were just as likely to be above the fold as they were to be below it. If scrolling below the fold was a source of frustration, we would have expected to see some sort of negative correlation between first clicks below the fold and success, but we didn't.

FIGURE 6.4

The Fidelity site went
to great lengths to
design pages that
display completely
above the fold. We
found no evidence to
suggest that this
strategy either helped
or hurt.

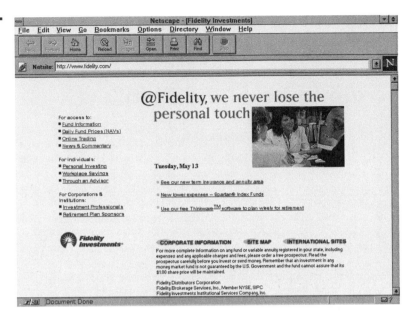

Rules as a Stopping Place

Users had some trouble with horizontal rules like the ones
shown in Figure 6.5, particularly when they fell at the fold.
Several sites used the lines to separate sections of content.
Repeatedly, users did not scroll below these lines, even
though they did scroll down other long pages.

The problem was most apparent with simple lines that
extend almost the full width of the page. We believe that
some users thought these were bottom of page indicators
or separators between "real" content and copyright-type
information.

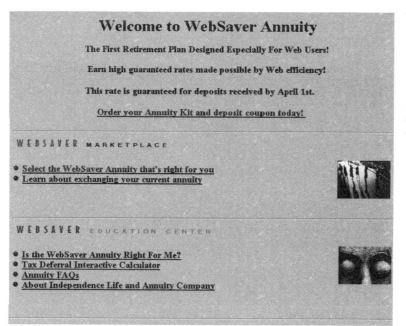

FIGURE 6.5

The WebSaver site uses a lot of horizontal rules. Some users did not scroll past them, especially when they fell at the fold.

Button Gravity

We also saw a phenomenon that we've come to call "button gravity." When working on a site that had multiple buttons on a page, like the Inc. site in Figure 6.6, users filled in one field, then scrolled to the bottom of the page and clicked the bottom-most button. It didn't matter that there was often a button right next to the field; users plummeted to the bottom of the page.

FIGURE 6.6

Users on the Inc. site filled in one field and hit the bottom-most Search button.

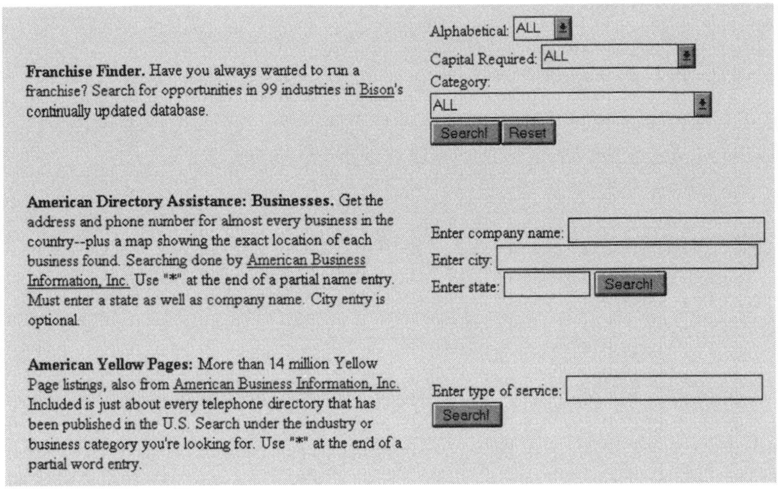

Alphabetical: ALL

Capital Required: ALL

Category:
ALL

[Search!] [Reset]

Franchise Finder. Have you always wanted to run a franchise? Search for opportunities in 99 industries in <u>Bison</u>'s continually updated database.

American Directory Assistance: Businesses. Get the address and phone number for almost every business in the country--plus a map showing the exact location of each business found. Searching done by <u>American Business Information, Inc.</u> Use "*" at the end of a partial name entry. Must enter a state as well as company name. City entry is optional.

Enter company name:

Enter city:

Enter state: [Search!]

American Yellow Pages: More than 14 million Yellow Page listings, also from <u>American Business Information, Inc.</u> Included is just about every telephone directory that has been published in the U.S. Search under the industry or business category you're looking for. Use "*" at the end of a partial word entry.

Enter type of service:
[Search!]

We also saw this happen frequently on the Travelocity site. Users were supposed to click the Submit button at the end of their last segment, as shown in Figure 6.7. Repeatedly, users entered their segments and dropped to the bottom button on the page.

FIGURE 6.7

Users filled in the two segments of their trip, then dropped to the bottom of the page and pressed the last Submit button. They didn't know they were supposed to press the button associated with the current field.

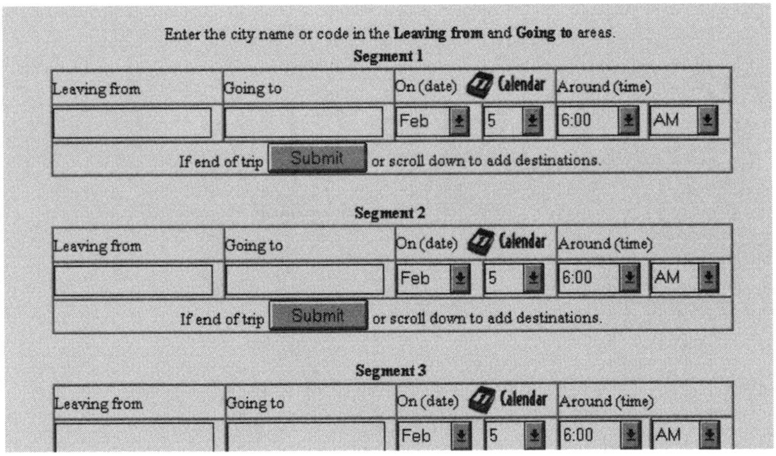

Enter the city name or code in the **Leaving from** and **Going to** areas.

Segment 1

Leaving from	Going to	On (date) 📅 Calendar	Around (time)
		Feb 5	6:00 AM

If end of trip [Submit] or scroll down to add destinations.

Segment 2

Leaving from	Going to	On (date) 📅 Calendar	Around (time)
		Feb 5	6:00 AM

If end of trip [Submit] or scroll down to add destinations.

Segment 3

Leaving from	Going to	On (date) 📅 Calendar	Around (time)
		Feb 5	6:00 AM

This behavior perplexed us until we thought about standard graphical user interfaces. Traditional interfaces rarely have buttons that operate on a single field. Usually there are OK and Cancel buttons in the bottom right that apply to the entire dialog box or form. When you think about it in that light, the users' actions make perfect sense!

CHAPTER 7

Graphic Design on the Web

Given the amount of information available about how to create good graphics for the web, we expected graphic design to affect the usability of our sites. In fact, we originally thought graphics were one of the three most important aspects of web site design, along with content and navigation.

We know better now. Although we measured every aspect of graphic design we could think of, we found no evidence that graphic design helps users retrieve information on a web site. It is worth noting, however, that we didn't study the marketing effects of graphics. Nor did we look at whether they make people more willing to return to a site. There may be correlations, but we didn't see them.

Two graphics issues did surprise us, however:

- In the sites we studied, download time was not an issue.
- Users could not concentrate when there was animation on the screen.

The Role of Graphic Design

Conventional wisdom holds that more graphical sites will be more interesting to users. The more interesting it is, the more time users spend there and, therefore, the more usable the site. It's a nice theory, but as far as we could find, it has no basis in reality.

The Edmund's site — a nearly "design-free zone" — finished ahead of many of our more graphically intense sites such as Disney, C|net, Inc., and Fidelity. Edmund's, as shown in Figure 7.1, is almost all text. The only graphics on the home page are three photos of books that the site is trying to sell. The site also includes thumbnail photographs of cars on the car description pages. If graphic design played a large role in success, we would have expected to see this site finish last.

FIGURE 7.1

The Edmund's site is definitely lacking in graphics and graphic design, but it finished at the top of our rankings. If graphic design played a large role in success, we wouldn't have seen these results.

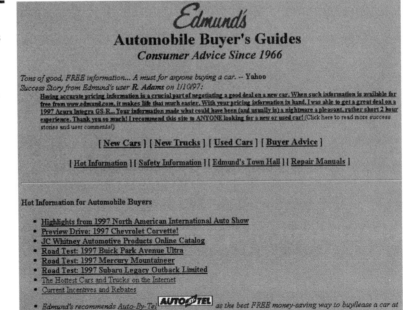

The Only Correlation: Link Color

The quality of graphic design seems to have little impact on users' ability to find and process information. We measured all the factors we could think of, including:

- Total number of graphics
- Size of graphics
- Number of content-based graphics
- Number of "fluff" graphics (that don't add to content)
- Number of graphic links
- Number of graphics with words in them
- Number of imagemaps
- Colors of links
- Colors of graphics
- Background color
- Presence of advertising
- Number of columns on the page
- Symmetrical versus asymmetrical layout

Sites with any of these graphic attributes did as well or as poorly as sites without them. For the most part, there was no correlation, either positive or negative, between graphic design elements and the users' success at finding information.

Of all the graphic design elements we looked at, the only one that is strongly tied to user success was use of browser-default link color. Netscape Navigator 3.0, for example, uses underlined blue text for links that the user hasn't followed, and underlined purple text for links that they have. Our theory is that use of the default colors is helpful because users don't have to relearn every time they go to a new site.

What's interesting about this is not the link color itself. Rather, this is the only attribute that correlates with success, and the correlation isn't even that strong. We would have expected other attributes to be significant also, but none were.

The long and short of it is that — except for link colors — we found no graphic element in this testing that made a big difference to the search for information, positively or negatively. Graphic elements per se did not seem to add to or detract from users' ability to find information.

Download Time

We've all heard the brouhaha about download speed and the World Wide Wait. We expected download time to affect the usability of sites. But after watching dozens of users with 28.8 modems, we didn't see major problems because of download time.

Keep in mind, however, that we tested high-use, professionally designed sites. Download time may have already been minimized. Several users did, however, experience problems with server time — when they had to wait to connect to a web server.

When users thought an image would have interesting content, they would wait for it to load. When they thought the image was purely decorative, like those in Figure 7.2, they were less patient.

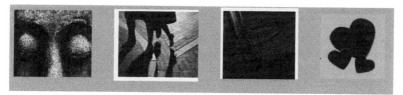

To Wait or Not to Wait

Most users followed the same pattern when they went to a new page. As the page was loading, they skimmed the text and any alternate text for graphics, such as that shown in Figure 7.3. If they found an interesting link in the text, they jumped before the graphics had a chance to load. Otherwise, when the page was fully loaded, they scrolled top to bottom and back to figure out what to do next.

FIGURE 7.2

Take our window-dressing graphics quiz! Each of these graphics comes from a different site: Hewlett Packard, Travelocity, WebSaver, and Fidelity. Can you guess which graphic dresses which site? (The answer is on page 91 in Figure 7.8.)

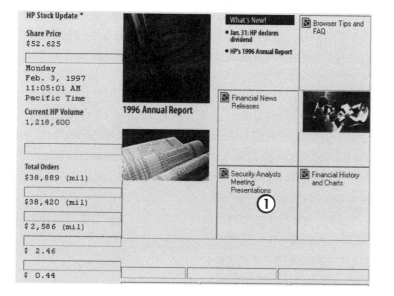

FIGURE 7.3

On this page from Hewlett Packard's site, users sometimes just skimmed the alternate text ① and left the page before it finished loading.

This caused problems for some users at the Hewlett Packard site. We asked users to find out what stock dividend the company paid last quarter. The answer was positioned

FIGURE 7.4

Hewlett Packard uses graphics as labels, so some of the heads do not load immediately. (The boxes are placeholders during loading.) Users did not know that ① was the answer they sought.

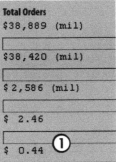

prominently on the Financial Online page, but the site uses lots of little images (without alternate text) for headers, as shown in Figure 7.4. Consequently, though the answer appeared quickly, users left the page before the labels appeared.

Because users didn't think the images would provide valuable content, they went to other sections of the page. Figure 7.5 shows what users would have seen if they had waited for the images to load.

FIGURE 7.5

If users had waited for all the images to load, they would have realized that they were already looking at the dividend.

Total Orders	
$38,889 (mil)	
Net Revenue	
$38,420 (mil)	
Net Earnings	
$ 2,586 (mil)	
Earnings per Share	
$ 2.46	
Dividends per share	
$ 0.44	

Interestingly, some users claimed they'd wait for graphics to download if they thought the content would be useful. As one user said, "My patience depends on the value of the information." We rarely saw these people wait, however.

Users were particularly frustrated when they thought a graphic would add to the content, but it didn't. Certain graphics in the Hewlett Packard, Disney, and WebSaver sites fell into this category, but this was especially evident with one graphic from the Edmund's site. While this site was not graphically rich, it did contain thumbnail pictures of new car models. These images loaded slowly, but this didn't upset users. In fact the suspense seemed almost enjoyable, except in one case. Car manufacturers had not yet released pictures of one new model, so the site included a picture of a car with a concealing layer of cloth over it. Once the picture finally loaded, several users expressed frustration at having to wait for a picture with no value. (We can't even print some of their quotes!)

Animation and Movement

You can hardly move in some web sites today without having something pop, flash, or zoom at you. Animation is everywhere — both in advertisements and in the pages themselves. Users find this animation uniformly irritating. In fact, some users were so distracted by it that they could not even read the other text on the screen.

In fairness, we need to say that we're sure someone somewhere is using animation to actually enhance the information retrieval or reading process, but we didn't see it. None of the sites we tested actually used animation to support the content. The animation was gratuitous — it could be removed and nothing would be lost from the content of the site.

The Distraction of Movement

Animation makes it considerably harder for users to read or skim. Repeatedly, we saw users fight the distraction of the movement in order to concentrate on the content. For example, the Disney home page had an animated graphic of a young girl dancing, as shown in Figure 7.6. Users first tried to scroll the animation off the page, and when they couldn't, actually covered it up with their hands so they could read the rest of the text.

FIGURE 7.6

Some users were so annoyed by animated images like this one that they covered them up!

Subsequently, when Disney revised the site, the designers kept the image, but eliminated the animation.

Users had a similar reaction to one of the ads on the Fidelity site. The animation appeared in the upper left corner of the screen, and showed a series of words and images spinning and jumping out toward the user, as shown in Figure 7.7. Several users covered this up so they could focus on the text.

Other sites had animation, and users commented on it, but they didn't seem to find it as annoying as on the sites described above.

The Disney and Fidelity animations have two things in common. First, users could not scroll the animation off the screen because of its placement on the page. (At other sites, they could.) Second, these two animations simulated 3-D movement. The images became larger, giving the appearance of moving closer to the user. We suspect that one or both of these factors may have made these animations particularly annoying.

Movement in Ads

Advertisements generally contained the most movement, but users masked out the ads when searching for content. For example, one user who was trying find the lowest airline fare to London repeatedly ignored an animated ad that offered "Find the lowest fare to anywhere." When asked about this after failing to complete the task, the user said

"That's what that ad was? I couldn't look at it." This user didn't see this ad at all, even though it contained the answer.

This indicates to us that animated ads may not communicate their message to the user. But the dozens of studies about banner advertising suggest that animated ads are more effective at click-through — getting users to follow the link to the web site being advertised — than non-animated ads.

Why the stark difference? It appears that surfing (where click-through is critical to commercial success) is significantly different from information retrieval. We believe that designing for one may actually hurt a design for the other. Most web designers don't think of this distinction. This could complicate web site design, given that it may not be possible to design one site for both purposes.

FIGURE 7.8

Here are the answers to the window-dressing graphics quiz on page 87.

CHAPTER 8

User Preference

In doing software usability testing, we've found that users usually prefer the application that they find most usable. We expected the same to be true of web sites, but it's not.

After users had worked with several sites, we asked them which site they liked best and which site they disliked most. Table 8.1 shows the rankings. It also shows the rankings of sites in order of user success.

If user likes, success, and dislikes all measured the same thing, we would expect the sites to appear in the same order in each column of the table, but they don't.

TABLE 8.1

Here are our site
rankings based on
user success, user
likes, and user
dislikes. The farther
down a site is in each
column, the worse it
did.

	User Success	Users Like Most	Users Dislike Least
1	Edmund's	Travelocity	Tie: Edmund's, Olympic
2	Olympic	Olympic	
3	Hewlett Packard	Hewlett Packard	Travelocity
4	WebSaver	Tie: Edmund's, Disney (new)	Hewlett Packard
5	Travelocity		WebSaver
6	Inc. (new)	Disney (old)	Inc. (old)
7	Disney (new)	Inc. (new)	Disney (new)
8	Inc. (old)	C|net	Fidelity
9	C|net	WebSaver	Tie: C|net, Disney (old)
10	Fidelity	Tie: Fidelity, Inc. (old)	
11	Disney (old)		Inc. (new)

Success and User *Likes*

Asking users if they like a site is not a good indication of
whether they can successfully use it, as shown by the
differences in columns one and two.

For example, notice where WebSaver appears — it was one
of the least-liked sites (ranking ninth), but users were fairly
successful with it. (It ranked fourth for user success.) Also

consider Travelocity. It was the site users liked best, but only ranked fifth in terms of user success.

We asked users *why* they liked the sites they chose. Uniformly they said they liked sites the best that had content that was interesting and relevant to them. For example, users liked Travelocity because of its potential for helping them find low airfares and fun travel destinations. They liked the Olympic site because we conducted our study shortly after the 1996 Summer Olympic games, when interest in the results was still quite high.

Success and User *Dislikes*

Interestingly, columns two and three (Users Like Most and Users Dislike Least) are not the same, implying that they measure different things. In fact, the Users Dislike Least column more closely matches the rankings in the User Success column. Notice that no site differs by more than two slots between these columns.

When users said they disliked a site, their reasons usually related to some significant difficulty in using it. Therefore, if a user *dislikes* a site, it does seem to indicate a usability problem.

Web Sites *Are* Different

In the past, when we have conducted usability studies that compared similar software and hardware products, we found that user preference is usually strongly correlated to success in using the product. In other words, the product users say they like best is usually the product they found easiest to use.

With web sites, it's a different story. The sites users liked were often different from the ones they could successfully use. In this respect, web sites are different from conventional software.

These results are disturbing because they imply that designing a site that users like and designing a site that they can use may be conflicting goals. On the other hand, these results may mean simply that good content is so important to users that other factors are secondary. In any case, we cannot depend on user satisfaction to indicate a usable web site.

Part 2:
Site Scrapbook

This section gives you a guided tour of the sites we studied, beginning with the site that scored best (Edmund's) and continuing down the rankings.

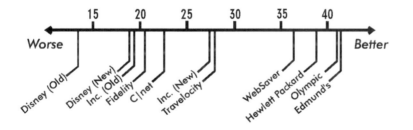

There's one exception: The Olympic site, which finished second in our study, was taken down before we got any pictures. Although we tried contacting the creator of the web site, we couldn't gain access to it.

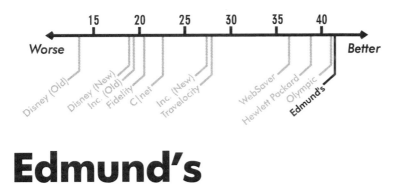

CHAPTER 9

Edmund's

The Edmund's site (www.edmunds.com) is a resource for consumers who want to research and purchase cars and trucks. This is a "shovelware" site: It contains all the content from Edmund's printed publications and then some.

The success of the Edmund's site surprised us. The site is mostly text, with no graphic design. Users rated this site highly for its authoritativeness and quality of information, and they successfully used it to find information.

We believe the success of this site has to do with its long, descriptive links, which help users predict where they will go and what information they will find there. Edmund's also does a good job of providing cross-links to related content. The site does lack a search facility. This caused one user to give up.

TABLE 9.1

We used these
questions to test the
Edmund's site.

Question Type	Example Question
Simple Fact	Can you get a new Honda Accord for under $15,000?
Comparison of Facts	Which truck has the best pickup speed, a 4WD Jeep Grand Cherokee Limited or a Toyota Land Cruiser?
Judgment	Your niece is considering buying a used Ford F-10 pickup. From the perspective of safety, is that a good idea?
Comparison of Judgment	In your opinion, what's the best new convertible for under $20,000?

FIGURE 9.1

The Edmund's home
page is essentially
one big table of
contents. This is only
the top third of the
page.

Edmund's
Automobile Buyer's Guides
Consumer Advice Since 1966

Tons of good, FREE information... A must for anyone buying a car. – Yahoo
Success Story from Edmund's user R. Adams on 1/10/97:
> Having accurate pricing information is a crucial part of negotiating a good deal on a new car. When such information is available for free from www.edmund.com, it makes life that much easier. With your pricing information in hand, I was able to get a great deal on a 1997 Acura Integra GS-R... Your information made what could have been (and usually is) a nightmare a pleasant, rather short 2 hour experience. Thank you so much! I recommend this site to ANYONE looking for a new or used car! (Click here to read more success stories and user comments!)

[**New Cars**] [**New Trucks**] [**Used Cars**] [**Buyer Advice**]

[Hot Information] [Safety Information] [Edmund's Town Hall] [Repair Manuals]

Hot Information for Automobile Buyers

- Highlights from 1997 North American International Auto Show
- Preview Drive: 1997 Chevrolet Corvette!
- JC Whitney Automotive Products Online Catalog
- Road Test: 1997 Buick Park Avenue Ultra
- Road Test: 1997 Mercury Mountaineer
- Road Test: 1997 Subaru Legacy Outback Limited
- The Hottest Cars and Trucks on the Internet
- Current Incentives and Rebates
- *Edmund's recommends Auto-By-Tel* **AUTO🚗TEL** *as the best FREE money-saving way to buy/lease a car at a full-service dealer near you!*

New Car Information *(For New Pickups, Vans or Sport Utilities, see below!)*

NEW CARS PRICES & REVIEWS ⟵ Click here for Car Prices!

- Edmund's Complete, Updated, NEW CARS Book Content
  Over 565 Models: *MSRP and Dealer Invoice Prices, Standard and Optional Equipment, Specifications, Reviews, etc.*

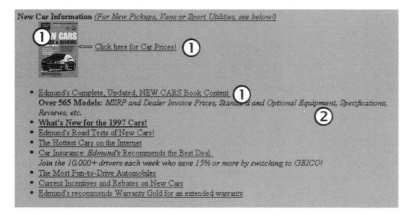

FIGURE 9.2

The success of the Edmund's site may be due to its use of long, descriptive, redundant links.

① These three links take users to exactly the same place. People used all three in our tests.

② Not only are the links long, but many of them are followed by a further description of content. Users liked the long, descriptive links. As one user said, "I know what I'm going to get." Another user commented that he sometimes got useful information just by reading the descriptions even if he didn't end up clicking the link.

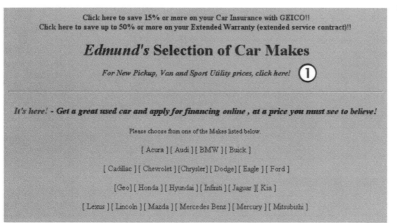

FIGURE 9.3

It seems the site designers anticipated cases where the user might need to access related information.

① Is a sport utility vehicle a car or a truck? If users don't know, it doesn't matter, because Edmund's provides a link to sport utilities from the car page.

FIGURE 9.4

This detail from the
Pontiac Sunfire page
shows links to
competing models,
which theoretically
allows users to
compare
alternatives.
However, no one
used these links.

Last year, we drove a Sunfire SE Convertible for a week, and only had complaints about excessive body roll, an ineffective climate control system when the top was down and the windows were up, and very weak stereo speakers. Otherwise, our Twin Cam 5-speed test car was a hoot, prompting a friend with a 1991 Mustang LX 5.0 automatic to quip "I better get some different gears in this thing. I can't have Sunfires keeping up with me." Best of all, our well-equipped test car came in under $20,000.

We think the Sunfire has what it takes to succeed in the crowded compact marketplace. If anything, the Sunfire makes a strong argument against purchasing its slightly larger stablemate, the Grand Am. If a sporty coupe, sedan or convertible is on your shopping list, check into the Sunfire.

COMPETING MODELS

Ford Mustang Convertible
Chevrolet Cavalier LS Convertible
Chrysler Sebring JX Convertible
Volkswagen Cabrio
Toyota Paseo Convertible

Return to Vehicle Information Menu

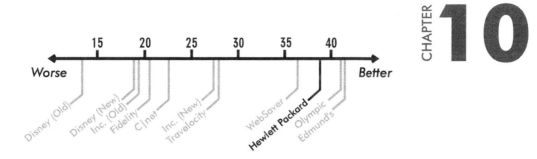

CHAPTER 10

Hewlett Packard

The Hewlett Packard site (www.hp.com) did well in our study. Unlike Edmund's, the Hewlett Packard site does have a professionally designed look.

We believe that part of the success of the Hewlett Packard site lies in how different its links are from each other. If it is true that users navigate "in the moment," well-differentiated links increase the chances that users will stay on the correct path to their desired information.

In testing this site, we noticed a drawback to using GIF images as text headers — users didn't always wait for the page to finish loading before they clicked a link. This can cause users to miss the answer they're looking for.

Question Type	Example Question
Simple Fact	How much was the last dividend payment?
Comparison of Facts	Which printer would be most difficult to move, the HP4V or 5M?
Judgment	Would Hewlett Packard be a good place to work?
Comparison of Judgment	Which HP ScanJet printer would be better for the things you do at home?

TABLE 10.1

These are the questions we used to test the Hewlett Packard site.

FIGURE 10.1

Hewlett Packard's home page has terse but easily distinguishable links. Many links are also duplicated.

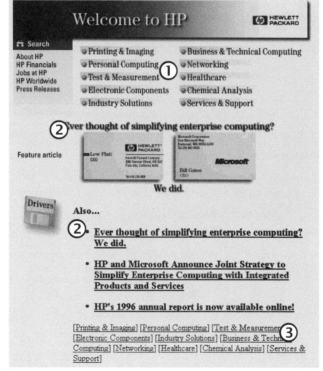

① Hewlett Packard's links, though terse, seemed to let users differentiate among them. Interestingly, several users initially thought these links were ads.

② Redundant links.

③ These text links were hard for some users to read.

FIGURE 10.2

Sometimes the order in which text and images appear can affect user behavior. This is what this page looks like when it is partially loaded.

① Some of the image links display alternate text while the page loads.

② Some users couldn't find this dividend because they left the page before the headers finished displaying.

FIGURE 10.3

The same page after it finishes loading. Notice that it's now clear what the numbers mean.

FIGURE 10.4

Hewlett Packard's
search screen is
straightforward,
but...

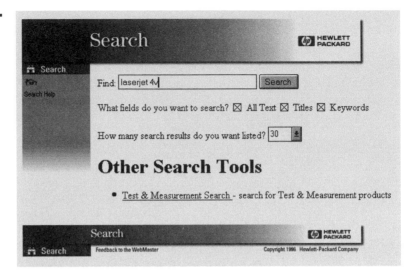

FIGURE 10.5

...the search results
are cryptic. They
even included
duplicates and
documents in
languages other than
English.

① Users had no idea what the relevancy numbers told them.

Printing & Imaging HEWLETT PACKARD

Choose The HP Printer That's Right For You

Whether your needs are simple or complex, there's an HP printer that's right for you. HP printers offer more for the money than any other printers on the market. And each is backed by the assurance of HP's industry-leading warranty. HP printers are the right choice every time!

What Are Your Printing Needs?

Answer the following questions to find the HP printer that will best meet your needs. When you have answered all the questions, click the **Find Printers** button below for a list of the printers that match your needs.

Step 1. **What kind of computer(s)** will the printer be connected to? (select all that apply)
☐ DOS ☒ Microsoft Windows ☐ OS/2 ☐ Macintosh ☐ UNIX(R)

Step 2. **Black or black and color** printing?
[black printing only ▾]

Step 3. **How many people** will share the printer?
[small group ▾]

Step 4. [Find Printers]

Figure 10.6

Hewlett Packard recently added these screens to let users find and compare printers. We have not tested this approach, but most web sites support comparisons poorly, if at all.

HP Printers For You

Here are the HP printers that best match your requirements:

- Microsoft Windows
- black printing only
- small group

or, you may go back and change your requirements. The printers in the table below are arranged in order from lowest price to highest.

Cost	HP Printer	Platforms Supported	Black Print Quality	Print Tech	Print Speed (pages/min) B/W color	Page per Mont
$	LaserJet 6P	S S S O O	*****	Laser	8	12,0
$	LaserJet 6MP	S S S S O	*****	Laser	8	12,0
$$	LaserJet 5P	S S S O O	*****	Laser	6	12,0
$$	LaserJet 5MP	S S S S O	*****	Laser	6	12,0
$$	LaserJet 5	S S S O O	*****	Laser	12	35,
$$	LaserJet 5N	S S S O S	*****	Laser	12	35,
$$$	LaserJet 4V	S S S O O	*****	Laser	16	50,
$$$$	LaserJet 4MV	S S S S S	*****	Laser	16	50,

```
                  | | | | |
         DOS-+ | | | +- Unix
         Win----+ | +-----Mac
         OS/2------+
Legend
------
Platforms Supported:
S: Standard
O: Optional
-: Unsupported
```

Figure 10.7

Although we did not test this, these search results might make it easier for the user to do a side-by-side comparison of potentially suitable printers.

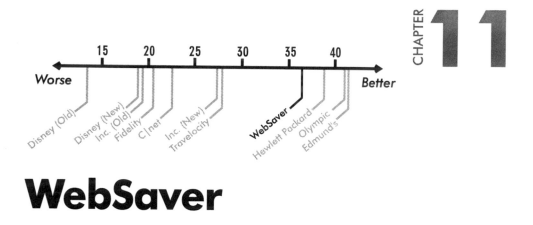

CHAPTER 11

WebSaver

WebSaver (www.websaver.com) is the smallest site we tested, and this may have helped users find information quickly. In particular, the Frequently Asked Questions (FAQ) page proved to be useful. No one seemed hampered by the lack of a search facility.

A couple of aspects of the graphic design caused minor problems. Some of the site's images had nothing to do with annuities, and users expressed mild annoyance at waiting for them to download. Also, the horizontal rules on the home page seemed to cause some users to stop scrolling prematurely.

Although WebSaver is intended to help users choose which annuity is right for them, the site's design does not facilitate comparing the four annuities side by side.

TABLE 11.1

These are the
questions we used to
test the WebSaver
site.

Question Type	Example Question
Simple Fact	What is an annuity?
Comparison of Facts	Of the four plans offered, which one will give your aunt the best return on her investment in the first year?
Judgment	Evaluate the company. Would you recommend this company to your aunt?
Comparison of Judgment	Your aunt has $10,000 to put into an annuity. Which plan do you think would be best for her?

FIGURE 11.1

The "Is the WebSaver
annuity right for me?"
link led to this form.
Because of the nature
of the questions,
users saw the form as
a marketing tool
rather than something
that would help them
make a choice.

Is the WebSaver Annuity Right For Me?

The WebSaver Annuity may not be the right retirement savings choice for everyone. Answer these five questions to see if the WebSaver Annuity may be right for you.

1. Are you already contributing the maximum amount you can to tax-qualified retirement plans for which you qualify - such as IRA, 401(k), 403(b), or KEOGH plans?

   ○ YES ○ NO

2. Are you concerned that your current retirement savings program may not be sufficient to provide real financial security and independence for your retirement?

   ○ YES ○ NO

3. Do you realistically have at least $2,000 you can set aside for retirement --- money that you don't expect to need for upcoming bills?

   ○ YES ○ NO

4. Do you already own an annuity?

   ○ YES ○ NO

5. WebSaver Annuity pays competitive guaranteed fixed rates that reflect the efficiency of direct World Wide Web distribution. Would you consider an attractive tax deferred fixed rate instrument for your supplemental retirement savings?

   ○ YES ○ NO

[Proceed] [Clear My Answers]

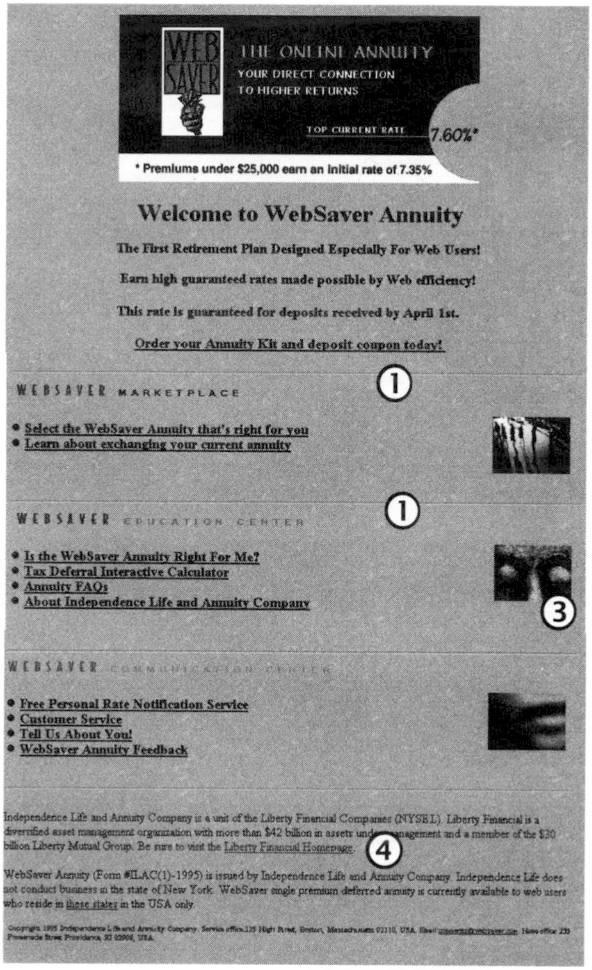

FIGURE 11.2

WebSaver's home page showed some subtle problems with graphic design.

① These horizontal rules may have caused some users to stop scrolling prematurely.

② Two similar links. Which one should the user click?

③ This art had nothing to do with annuities. The wait to download these images annoyed some users.

④ The link to Liberty Financial seemed to boost the users' confidence in the quality of its information.

Figure 11.3

WebSaver offers four annuties, but the user must scroll up and down to compare them. There is no way to view them all at once.

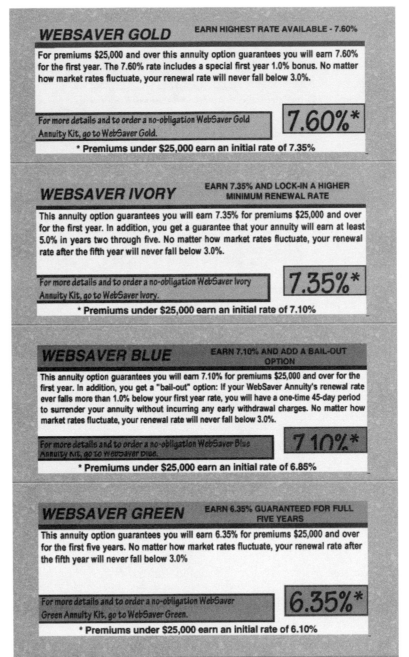

WEBSAVER GOLD   EARN HIGHEST RATE AVAILABLE - 7.60%

For premiums $25,000 and over this annuity option guarantees you will earn 7.60% for the first year. The 7.60% rate includes a special first year 1.0% bonus. No matter how market rates fluctuate, your renewal rate will never fall below 3.0%.

For more details and to order a no-obligation WebSaver Gold Annuity Kit, go to WebSaver Gold.

7.60%*

* **Premiums under $25,000 earn an initial rate of 7.35%**

WEBSAVER IVORY   EARN 7.35% AND LOCK-IN A HIGHER MINIMUM RENEWAL RATE

This annuity option guarantees you will earn 7.35% for premiums $25,000 and over for the first year. In addition, you get a guarantee that your annuity will earn at least 5.0% in years two through five. No matter how market rates fluctuate, your renewal rate after the fifth year will never fall below 3.0%.

For more details and to order a no-obligation WebSaver Ivory Annuity Kit, go to WebSaver Ivory.

7.35%*

* **Premiums under $25,000 earn an initial rate of 7.10%**

WEBSAVER BLUE   EARN 7.10% AND ADD A BAIL-OUT OPTION

This annuity option guarantees you will earn 7.10% for premiums $25,000 and over for the first year. In addition, you get a "bail-out" option: If your WebSaver Annuity's renewal rate ever falls more than 1.0% below your first year rate, you will have a one-time 45-day period to surrender your annuity without incurring any early withdrawal charges. No matter how market rates fluctuate, your renewal rate will never fall below 3.0%.

For more details and to order a no-obligation WebSaver Blue Annuity Kit, go to WebSaver Blue.

7.10%*

* **Premiums under $25,000 earn an initial rate of 6.85%**

WEBSAVER GREEN   EARN 6.35% GUARANTEED FOR FULL FIVE YEARS

This annuity option guarantees you will earn 6.35% for premiums $25,000 and over for the first five years. No matter how market rates fluctuate, your renewal rate after the fifth year will never fall below 3.0%

For more details and to order a no-obligation WebSaver Green Annuity Kit, go to WebSaver Green.

6.35%*

* **Premiums under $25,000 earn an initial rate of 6.10%**

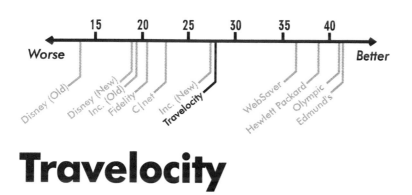

CHAPTER 12

Travelocity

Travelocity (www.travelocity.com) lets users make travel reservations and do research on recreational activities at destinations worldwide.

Travelocity was created by Sabre, which also develops dedicated reservation systems for travel agents and airlines. Some of the concepts in the site, such as trip segments, are familiar to travel agents but were unfamiliar to users (a newer version of the site now lets users specify round-trips). There are also several different ways to find airfares and users weren't sure which path to choose.

Travelocity requires users to register to complete their search for airfares. The registration screen was a surprise to users. Many were reluctant to type in personal information before they had committed to buying anything.

TABLE 12.1

These are the
questions we used to
test the Travelocity
site.

Question Type	Example Question
Simple Fact	Find a place to take your nine-year-old niece horseback riding.
Comparison of Facts	You've decided to take your niece to either England or Nevada to perfect her riding skills. Assume you're leaving on May 15 and staying for two weeks. Which flight is cheaper?
Judgment	Do you think your niece would enjoy a trip to Hampton Court?
Comparison of Judgment	Pick a show to take your niece to while you're in London.

FIGURE 12.1

The top of
Travelocity's home
page presents the
site's four main
sections. (The
bottom half appears
in Figure 12.2.)

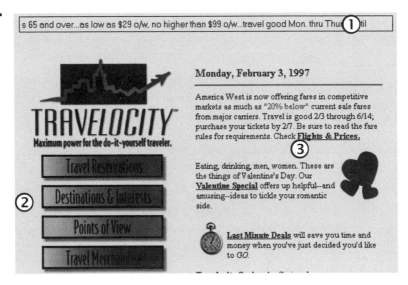

① The moving banner was distracting. Users often scrolled it off the screen.

② These buttons are well-differentiated. Different users all chose the same button to start each task.

③ Users skimmed the "news" but never found it relevant to their tasks. It just took time.

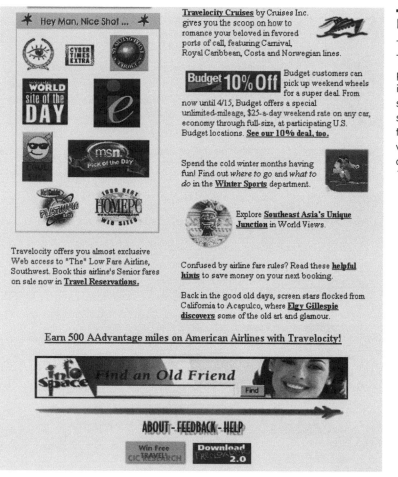

Travelocity Cruises by Cruises Inc. gives you the scoop on how to romance your beloved in favored ports of call, featuring Carnival, Royal Caribbean, Costa and Norwegian lines.

Budget customers can pick up weekend wheels for a super deal. From now until 4/15, Budget offers a special unlimited-mileage, $25-a-day weekend rate on any car, economy through full-size, at participating U.S. Budget locations. See our 10% deal, too.

Spend the cold winter months having fun! Find out *where to go* and *what to do* in the Winter Sports department.

Explore Southeast Asia's Unique Junction in World Views.

Travelocity offers you almost exclusive Web access to "The" Low Fare Airline, Southwest. Book this airline's Senior fares on sale now in Travel Reservations.

Confused by airline fare rules? Read these helpful hints to save money on your next booking.

Back in the good old days, screen stars flocked from California to Acapulco, where Elgy Gillespie discovers some of the old art and glamour.

Earn 500 AAdvantage miles on American Airlines with Travelocity!

Find an Old Friend — Find

ABOUT - FEEDBACK - HELP

Win Free TRAVEL!

Download 2.0

FIGURE 12.2

The remainder of Travelocity's home page presents information on special offers and shows the awards that the site has won. (The top half appears in Figure 12.1.)

FIGURE 12.3

This screen appears when the user selects "Travel Reservations" from the home page. Users had trouble deciding which of three similar links to choose to research round-trip fares.

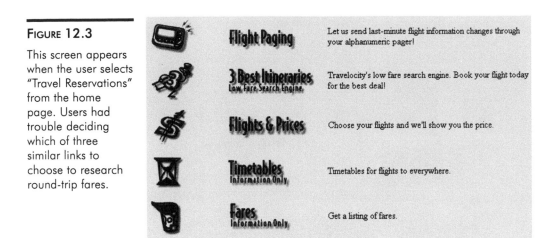

Flight Paging	Let us send last-minute flight information changes through your alphanumeric pager!
3 Best Itineraries Low Fare Search Engine	Travelocity's low fare search engine. Book your flight today for the best deal!
Flights & Prices	Choose your flights and we'll show you the price.
Timetables Information Only	Timetables for flights to everywhere.
Fares Information Only	Get a listing of fares.

FIGURE 12.4

Registration was a surprise and a show-stopper. Users weren't sure what to do. The site would not let them continue without registering.

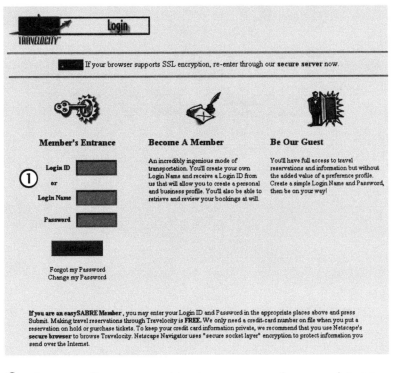

① Occasionally, a user would enter a name and password, just to see if it would work.

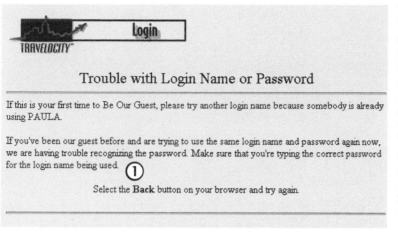

Login

TRAVELOCITY

Trouble with Login Name or Password

If this is your first time to Be Our Guest, please try another login name because somebody is already using PAULA.

If you've been our guest before and are trying to use the same login name and password again now, we are having trouble recognizing the password. Make sure that you're typing the correct password for the login name being used. ①

Select the **Back** button on your browser and try again.

① This error message doesn't give any advice on how to pick a unique name.

Airport Atlas — Gives you airport codes and can find the closest airports to your destination.

Enter the city name or code in the **Leaving from** and **Going to** areas.

Segment 1

Leaving from	Going to	On (date) 📅 **Calendar**	Around (time)
		Apr ▾ 25 ▾	6:00 ▾ AM ▾
① Click here ☐ for a **Round Trip** and enter ② date:		Apr ▾ 25 ▾	6:00 ▾ AM ▾
	If this is the end of the trip Submit or scroll down to add destinations.		

Segment 2

Leaving from	Going to	On (date) 📅 **Calendar**	Around (time)
		Apr ▾ 25 ▾	6:00 ▾ AM ▾
	If this is the end of th ② Submit or scroll down to add destinations.		

Segment 3

| Leaving from | Going to | On (date) 📅 **Calendar** | Around (time) |

① During our study, Travelocity changed this search to let users specify round-trips instead of segments. This newer method works better.

② The Submit buttons apply only to the segment immediately above, but some users scrolled down to the bottom of the page and clicked the last Submit button (what we call *button gravity*).

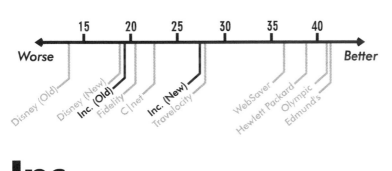

Inc.

Like the magazine of the same name, the Inc. site
(www.inc.com) offers articles and resources for small
businesses.

Inc. seems to take a *shell* approach to site design, since the
home page has many generic links, such as <u>databases</u>. It was
after watching users struggle with this site (and C|net, which
also takes a shell approach) that we began to doubt the
effectiveness of this approach. Users sometimes didn't know
which path to explore, and we think that the terse, non-
descriptive links may make it harder to choose.

Inc. redesigned its site halfway through our study. The
redesigned version has less white-space and fewer embedded
links. The redesigned version did slightly better than its
predecessor.

TABLE 13.1

These are the
questions we used to
test the Inc. site.

Question Type	Example Question
Simple Fact	What is the fax number of the Greater Boston Chamber of Commerce?
Comparison of Facts	Which is closer to your house, the Massachusetts Small Business Administration District office or Branch office?
Judgment	Your aunt has started a small business selling pottery. She would like to increase her advertising to attract new customers. Would it be helpful if she attended the April 1997 conference held in Phoenix?
Comparison of Judgment	What book would you choose to help your aunt advertise her business on the world wide web?

FIGURE 13.1

Inc. has a large
number of
resources, each with
its own search
facility. Users didn't
know which search
engine to use, or
whether they could
use more than one
at a time.

① It wasn't unusual for users to fill out fields for one database...

② ...but click the Search button for another. They were surprised by the search results, which were meaningless because they weren't from the search area the user wanted. Most users who had this problem didn't realize they had clicked the wrong button.

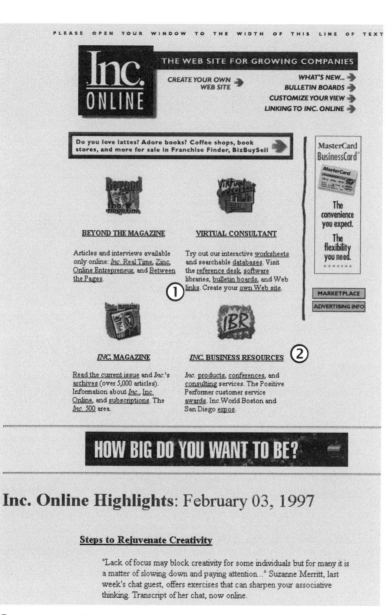

FIGURE 13.2

The Inc. home page is a shell. The links are high-level and generic, so that their content can change while the link remains the same. Users didn't know which link to select.

① Embedded links like these have a negative effect on user success.

② When looking up a fax number, users most often clicked here. They were surprised to get a list of Inc. magazine products and services. Fax numbers can be found in <u>databases</u>.

FIGURE 13.3

The revised Inc. home page, which did somewhat better. Note that there are fewer embedded links and less white-space.

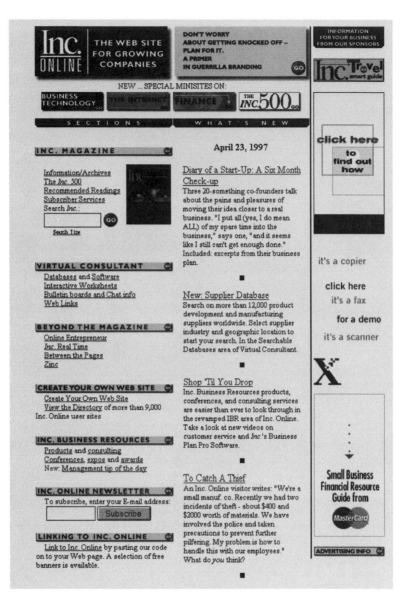

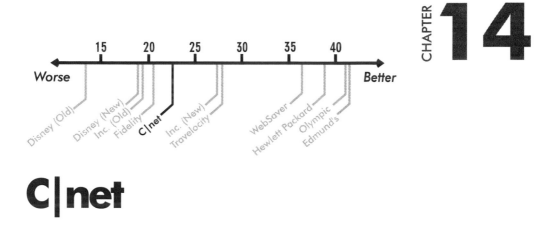

CHAPTER 14

C|net

The C|net site (www.cnet.com) provides technology re-
sources and information, including articles, product reviews,
and links to many other sites. The site is updated daily.

The C|net site is a shell: the left-hand side of its home page
contains many high-level links that do not change, although
the underlying content does.

When searching for specific information, users had trouble
deciding which link to follow. Users often explored the same
dead end more than once, and they had as much difficulty
answering the fourth question as they had with the first.

TABLE 14.1

These are the questions we used to test the C|net site.

Question Type	Example Question
Simple Fact	How much would it cost to purchase a C|net T-shirt?
Comparison of Facts	Which of the top three recommended digital cameras is the least expensive?
Judgment	Do you think "Wide World of Animals" would make a good gift for your nine-year-old niece?
Comparison of Judgment	If price is not an issue, which electronic dictionary software package would you choose for your aunt?

FIGURE 14.1

This is the top portion of C|net's home page (the bottom half appears in Figure 14.2). The middle and right columns are updated frequently, but the left column mostly stays the same (using a shell strategy). When users found an answer in one column, they tended to look in that column first to answer subsequent questions.

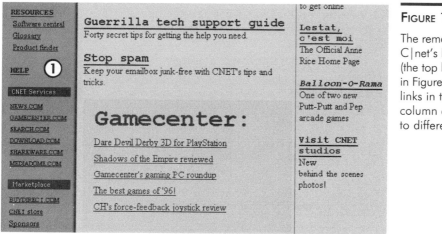

FIGURE 14.2

The remainder of C|net's home page (the top half appears in Figure 14.1). The links in the left-hand column are difficult to differentiate.

① Users had trouble deciding which link to choose to research a digital camera. Users explored Product finder, SEARCH.COM, All comparisons, Reviews, and BUYDIRECT.COM. In this case, the answer was found under All comparisons.

FIGURE 14.3

This page illustrates some of the navigational aids used in the C|net site. Unfortunately, users ignored them.

① No one used this link to return to the home page. They most often used the browser's Back button instead.

② These buttons take the user up one or two levels in the hierarchy. Users ignored these also.

FIGURE 14.4

It isn't clear what areas C|net's Product Finder covers or what it returns. Note that Product Finder has subsequently been removed from the site.

FIGURE 14.5

In this search, Product Finder returned the names of several manufacturers whose web sites had been reviewed by C|net. There was no indication that the C|net site contained several in-depth reviews of digital cameras, and not all the digital camera manufacturers were included in this list.

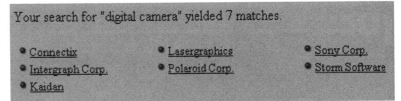

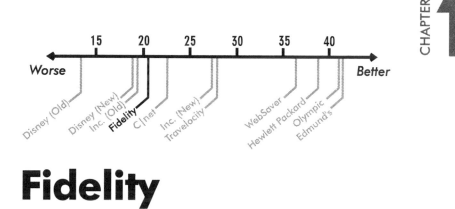

CHAPTER 15

Fidelity

The Fidelity site (www.fidelity.com) has information about Fidelity products and services for both individual and corporate investors.

Fidelity's pages are all fairly short, minimizing the need for scrolling, though the short page length didn't appear to have any effect on user success.

We did find some frame-related confusion. Users sometimes didn't notice that the content of the large frame changed when they clicked a link in the smaller left-hand frame. Sometimes they clicked repeatedly or perceived a problem with the site because they didn't see anything change.

The users who found the site map liked it and it seemed to help them choose links. Note that the site map only provides additional description of the home page links.

TABLE 15.1

These are the questions we used to test the Fidelity site.

Question Type	Example Question
Simple Fact	How many money market funds does Fidelity offer?
Comparison of Facts	Which fund has the better one-year return, the Market Index Fund or the Equity Income II Fund?
Judgment	Would stock funds be a good investment for your 49-year-old aunt's retirement?
Comparison of Judgment	Which international funds should your conservative aunt consider?

FIGURE 15.1

All of Fidelity's screens were fairly short, so that most of the page appeared "above the fold." We have no evidence that this either helped or hurt.

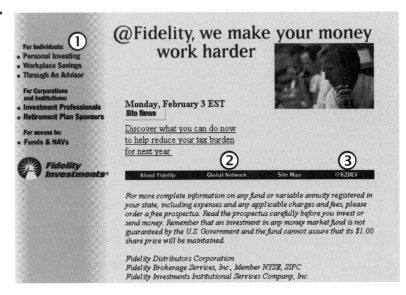

① The individual/corporate distinction helped users distinguish among the options.

② Users went here for information on international funds. Instead, this link leads to other Fidelity sites worldwide.

③ @82DEV is a sister site. Users didn't realize they were no longer on the original Fidelity site.

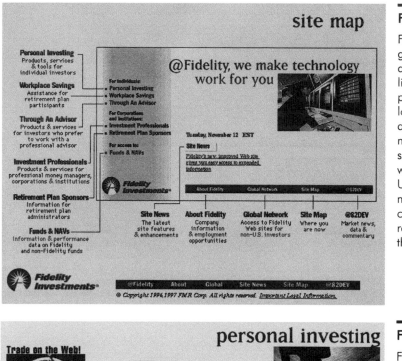

FIGURE 15.2

Fidelity's site map gives more description of the links on the home page. The users who looked at this page answered twice as many questions successfully as users who didn't see it. Users liked the site map. One user commented, "I'm really attached to this page."

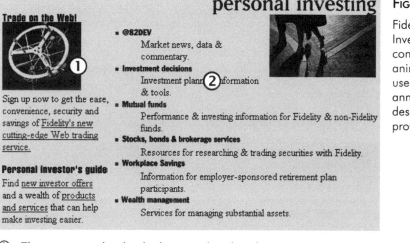

FIGURE 15.3

Fidelity's Personal Investing page contains an animated image that users found annoying, and link descriptions that proved to be useful.

① This rotating wheel, which is unrelated to the page content, distracted users. Since they couldn't scroll it off the screen, some users covered it with their hands.

② The descriptive text loads before the GIF image links. Users sometimes made their decision and tried to click the text before the links finished displaying.

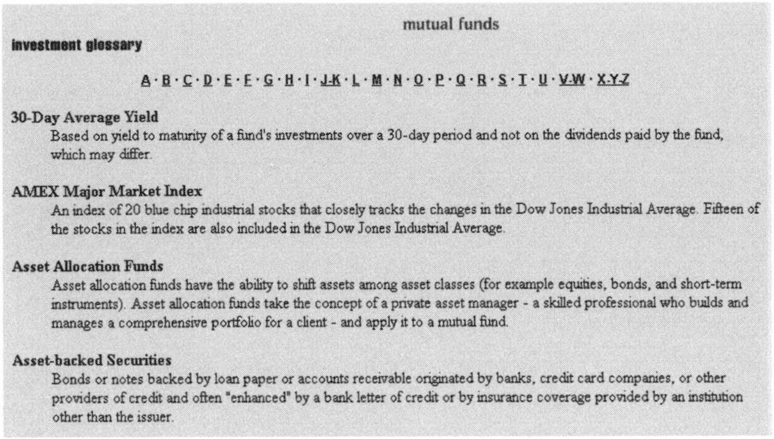

FIGURE 15.4

Fidelity's site included this dictionary to explain its terminology. However, this page took so long to come up that half of the users who tried to access it simply gave up.

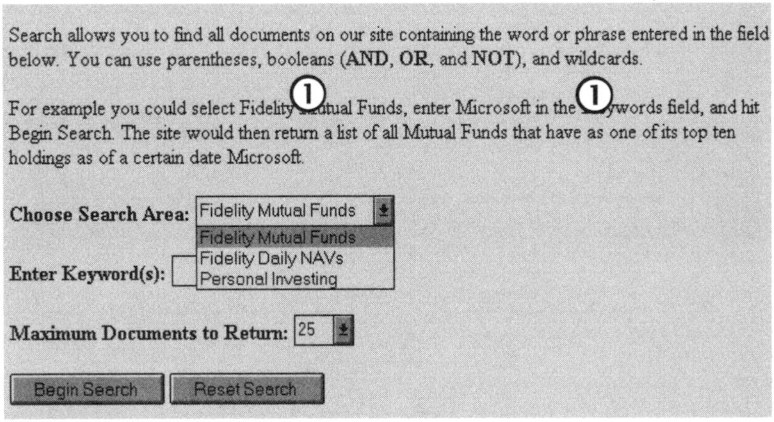

FIGURE 15.5

On Fidelity's search page, users didn't know what the search area terms meant, so they had difficulty deciding which to choose.

① Several users commented that they didn't know what booleans or wildcards were.

search

Choose Search Criteria: Personal Investing ▼

Enter Keyword(s): market index fund

Max Documents to Return: 25 ▼

[Begin Search] [Reset Search]

Here is the result of your search using the keyword(s) **"market index fund"**:

1: 223720.html
2: 223907.html
3: 223755.html
4: 221834.html
5: 223769.html
6: categories.html
7: 223781.html
8: Frequently Asked Questions About Investing
9: 221831.html
10: 223754.html
11: Frequently Asked Questions About Investing

FIGURE 15.6

The results returned by Fidelity's search engine were especially cryptic.

International Investing   frequently asked questions about investing

- I've been hearing a lot about international investing recently. Why is it suddenly so popular?
- How can I tell if international investing is right for me?
- How do international stock funds compare with domestic ones?

FIGURE 15.7

In contrast to the search results, the FAQ section had detailed information.

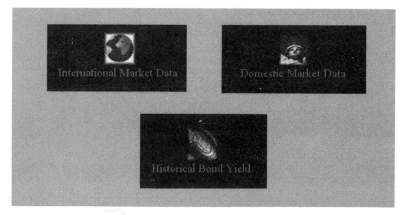

FIGURE 15.8

These flashing images from an animated ad were returned by the search engine as matches for "International."

FIGURE 15.9

The Fidelity site uses frames on some of its pages and sometimes they caused confusion.

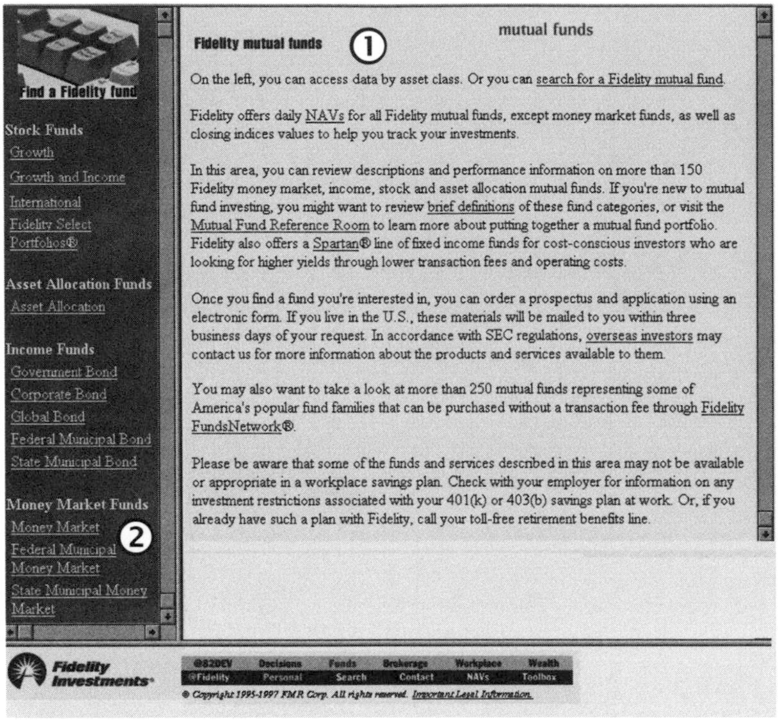

① Not all users noticed that the contents of the large frame changed when they clicked a link in the left frame. The changes were a bit more obvious when there was an image in the frame along with the text. Some users clicked on the same link again and nothing happened (because they were already there).

② One user didn't realize that these were wrapped links. He clicked on each wrapped part separately. He did not look at the URLs in the browser's status bar.

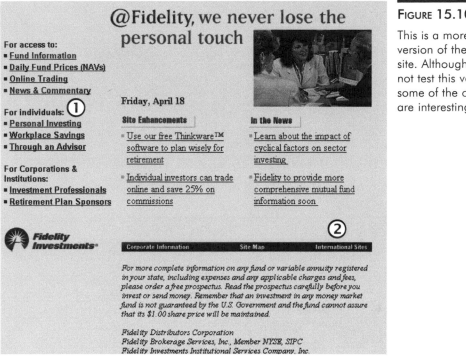

FIGURE 15.10

This is a more recent
version of the Fidelity
site. Although we did
not test this version,
some of the changes
are interesting.

① In a newer version of Fidelity's site, many of the image links
have been replaced with text links.

② The "Global Network" link is now called "International Sites"
and the link to the @82DEV site is gone.

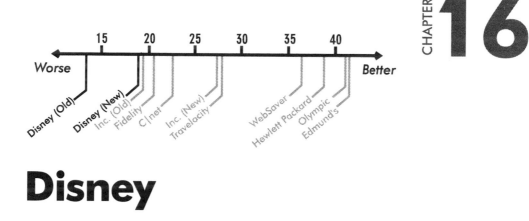

CHAPTER 16

Disney

Disney (www.disney.com) provides information on Disney's entire empire. We especially noticed problems with searching and interpretation of search results.

Users weren't aware that the 7,000-plus page Disney site encompasses several business areas, including amusement parks, television, videos, and merchandise. Once they followed a link to a particular area, such as Disneyland, users had trouble returning to the disney.com home page. Several users got "lost in Disneyland!"

Disney redesigned its site halfway through our study. The redesigned home page uses frames, and Disney made other changes as well. The new site did slightly better than the original, suggesting that frames didn't hurt its usability. On the other hand, we have no evidence that the frames helped.

	Question Type	Example Question
TABLE 16.1 These are the questions we used to test both versions of the Disney site.	Simple Fact	How much does a one-day pass to Walt Disney World cost?
	Comparison of Facts	Which wristwatch at the Disney store is the most expensive?
	Judgment	Which month has the best weather for a visit to Walt Disney World?
	Comparison of Judgment	Which Disney World hotel with access to the monorail would you choose to stay in?

FIGURE 16.1

The top portion of the old Disney home page is an imagemap. (The bottom appears in Figure 16.2.)

① Each page has a "mouse ears" link to get back to this home page, but only one user used it. Other users who wanted to return to this page could not figure out how to do so.

② Few users clicked on this imagemap. Most used either the text links beneath the imagemap or other text links on the page.

Education, fun local events: all at family.com

Win prizes! Trips! A car! A shopping spree! More!

Find that special valentine at The Disney Store Online!

BOOKS
Disney Publishing

HOME VIDEO
Aladdin and the King of Thieves
Toy Story
Walt Disney Home Video

MOVIES
101 Dalmatians
The Hunchback of Notre Dame
Walt Disney Pictures

MUSIC
Walt Disney Records

SHOPPING
The Disney Store Online
Send a Pooh Gram

SOFTWARE
Disney Interactive
Disney's Toy Story
Walt Disney World Explorer
Bill Nye the Science Guy

TELEVISION
The Disney Channel
Walt Disney Television

THEATER
Beauty & the Beast

THEME PARKS / VACATIONS
Disneyland
Walt Disney World
Disney Institute

THE WALT DISNEY COMPANY
Investor Information

INTERNATIONAL SITES

[Return to Top of Page]

find   help   e-mail   register   Created by Disney Online

PLEASE CLICK HERE FOR LEGAL RESTRICTIONS AND
TERMS OF USE APPLICABLE TO THIS SITE.
USE OF THIS SITE SIGNIFIES YOUR AGREEMENT TO THE TERMS OF USE.
© Disney. All rights reserved.

FIGURE 16.2

The remainder of the original Disney home page contained many links. (The top portion appears in Figure 16.1.)

① This animated image of a dancing girl annoyed users so much that many covered it with a hand.

② The three-column format forces many links to wrap. Users could not tell that The Disney Store and Online were the same link.

③ These links take the user to other home pages. There is no way to get from Disneyland to Walt Disney World, or vice versa. Although our test questions specified Disney World, many users followed the link to Disneyland and got lost.

FIGURE 16.3

This is the redesigned
Disney home page.
Note the addition of
frames and the
elimination of
imagemaps.

① No one used this graphical link to the home page, but users did
click Directory.

② The revised Disney home page uses lots of embedded links.

③ Few users used any of the links in the large frame when
searching for specific information. Instead, they used the links in
the lower right frame.

④ This page has three frames. When the user clicks a link in this
lower right frame, the large left frame changes. Because the
large frame includes graphics and the whole screen refreshes,
this interaction did not give users a problem, unlike the frames
in Fidelity's site.

⑤ Almost no one used the Table of Contents.

Walt Disney World Monorail [GO]

Type a name or description in the box above, or click on a link below.

BOOKS
Choose an online storybook
The Disney Publishing Catalog
Disney Publishing's featured books
Read-Along book & cassette sets

CALIFORNIA VACATIONS
What's New at Disneyland?
Disneyland park information
Magical places to stay at Disneyland
Helpful travel information

FLORIDA VACATIONS
Remember the Magic of Our 25th
Walt Disney World Theme Parks

ONSTAGE
All about "Beauty and the Beast"
"Beauty and the Beast" ticket info

SHOPPING
Visit The Disney Store Online
Send a Pooh Gram
Order Disney videos online
Shop for CD-ROMs at our store

SOFTWARE
Spot the Dalmatians CD-ROMs
Explore "Toy Story" CD-ROMs
Bill Nye's CD-ROM rules!
The CD-ROM of "Notre Dame"

FIGURE 16.4

The Disney search facility covers several areas of the site, but does not make this clear when the user initially specifies the search.

---

38 : Welcome to Disneyland
Welcome to Disneyland . . Press Release: . .INSIDE .OUT . ALL NEW "INSIDE OUT" OFFERS BEHIND THE SCENES LOOK AT WALT DISNEY WORLD AND DISNEYLAND . Disney Channel's New Series Premieres December 12 "Inside Out," the all-new weekly Disney Channel series that takes viewers behind the scenes at Walt Disney World in Florida, and Disneyland i...
(7014 bytes)

39 : Disney Institute Vacation Plans - Basic, Deluxe, World Choice Plans
Disney Institute Vacation Plans - Basic, Deluxe, World Choice Plans . . JANUARY THROUGH DECEMBER 1997 .(Rates are per person, based on adult double occupancy.) . .BASIC PLAN .Includes accommodations, Disney Institute programs and evening entertainment, One-Day/One-Park Ticket to any Walt Disney World
(7169 bytes)

40 : Resorts & Reservations
Resorts & Reservations . . . . Unlock the unique theming of any of the following selected Walt Disney World Resorts and you open a World of Disney Guest Benefits: early admission to a Disney Theme Park on selected days, complimentary Walt Disney World
(6420 bytes)

41 : Walt Disney World Vacation Packages
Walt Disney World Vacation Packages . . . . Choosing a Package makes vacation planning a breeze. They're worry-free, so you can devote all your time to enjoying the fun. Vacation packages feature Disney Resort hotels and give you exclusive benefits and privileges. Disney Institute Vacation Packages .Disney's Summer Magic Package . The best way to experie...
(5094 bytes)

42 : Walt Disney World - Blizzard Beach
Walt Disney World - Blizzard Beach . . . . Features. | .Hours. | .Restaurants. | .Location/Transportation. | .Tickets .As legend has it, Blizzard Beach was created by a freak winter storm that dropped snow over the western side of Walt Disney World property. Temperatures soared, however, and as water began to cascade down Mt. Gushmore, the first s...
(7798 bytes)

FIGURE 16.5

It is difficult to see how some of these search results relate to the monorail. And although the user specified Walt Disney World, some of the hits returned by the search engine appear to pertain to Disneyland.

FIGURE 16.6

Only at the bottom of the long list of search results does the user see what areas of the site were actually searched. At this point, the search facility lets users exclude areas and re-run the search.

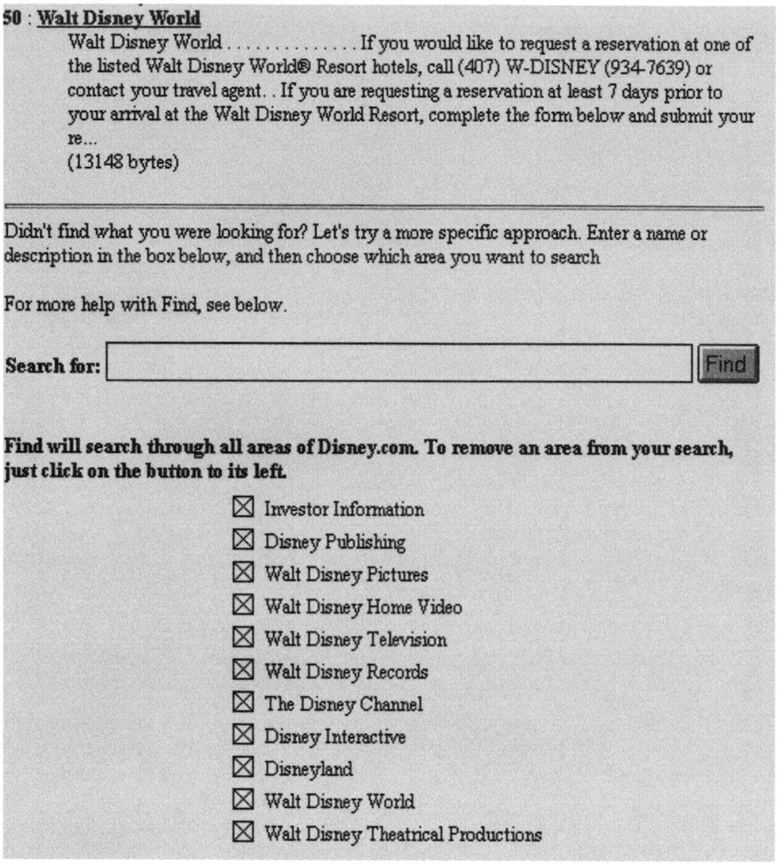

50 : <u>Walt Disney World</u>

Walt Disney World . . . . If you would like to request a reservation at one of the listed Walt Disney World® Resort hotels, call (407) W-DISNEY (934-7639) or contact your travel agent. . If you are requesting a reservation at least 7 days prior to your arrival at the Walt Disney World Resort, complete the form below and submit your re...
(13148 bytes)

Didn't find what you were looking for? Let's try a more specific approach. Enter a name or description in the box below, and then choose which area you want to search

For more help with Find, see below.

Search for: [   ] [Find]

Find will search through all areas of Disney.com. To remove an area from your search, just click on the button to its left.

- ☒ Investor Information
- ☒ Disney Publishing
- ☒ Walt Disney Pictures
- ☒ Walt Disney Home Video
- ☒ Walt Disney Television
- ☒ Walt Disney Records
- ☒ The Disney Channel
- ☒ Disney Interactive
- ☒ Disneyland
- ☒ Walt Disney World
- ☒ Walt Disney Theatrical Productions

Part 3:
Testing Sites

In this final part, we discuss how we measured and tested the sites in our study.

This isn't intended to be an overview of usability testing; there are plenty of other resources for that. Rather, you can use this information in two ways:

- *If you want to compare your web site directly to the ones we tested, you'll need to conduct your usability tests the same way we did.*

- *If you only want to make your site more usable and help users find information, you can adapt our methods to suit your purposes.*

CHAPTER 17

How We Tested Web Sites

This chapter describes the methods we used, including the types of questions we asked, the data we collected, and how we calculated the site rankings.

We assume that you already have some familiarity with usability testing. If not, two good books to look at are Penny Bauersfeld's Software by Design: Creating People Friendly Software (New York, M&T Books, 1994) and Jakob Nielsen's Usability Engineering (San Diego, Academic Press, 1993).

There are many different ways to conduct usability tests of web sites, depending on the purpose of the site. If you want to compare your web site directly against the sites we tested, you'll need to conduct your usability tests the same way we did. If you want to improve the usability of your own site to help users find information, you can adapt our methods to suit your purposes.

Types of Questions

We used four types of questions to study the ease of finding information on web sites. If you want to compare your site against the ones in our study, you'll need to create one question of each type.

1. Simple Fact Questions

The simplest type of question is a single fact retrieval, a question for which there is only one correct answer.

TABLE 17.1

Examples of simple fact questions

Inc.	What is the fax number for the Greater Boston Chamber of Commerce?
Fidelity	How many money market funds does Fidelity offer?
Hewlett Packard	How much was the last dividend payment?
C|net	How much would it cost to purchase a C|net T-shirt?

2. Judgment Questions

These questions are slightly more difficult, since the user must not only locate the answer, but then must analyze the information sufficiently to formulate an opinion based on it. Unlike a simple fact question, where there is one right answer, judgment questions require the user to decide whether he or she has found enough information to give a satisfactory answer.

Fidelity	Would stock funds be a good investment for your aunt's retirement?
Hewlett Packard	Would Hewlett Packard be a good place to work?
C|net	You would like to give your nine-year-old niece some new learning software. Do you think "Wide World of Animals" would make a good gift for her?
Disney	Which month has the best weather for a visit to Walt Disney World?

TABLE 17.2

Examples of judgment questions

3. Comparison of Fact Questions

In comparison questions, the user must research two or more facts, then compare them to arrive at the answer. These questions are more complicated than looking up one fact, because the user needs a way to remember each fact while looking up the rest.

Inc.	Which is closer to your house, the Massachusetts Small Business Association District Office or Branch Office?
Fidelity	Which fund has the better one-year return, the Market Index Fund or the Equity Income II Fund?
Olympics	Who had a faster 4 x 100 medley, the U.S. women's swim team or the Chinese men's swim team?
Disney	Which wristwatch at the Disney Store is the least expensive?

TABLE 17.3

Examples of comparison of fact questions

4. Comparison of Judgment Questions

The fourth type of question was the most complicated, involving both comparisons and judgments.

TABLE 17.4

Examples of comparison of judgment questions

Edmund's	In your opinion, what's the best new convertible for under $20,000?
Fidelity	Your aunt is very conservative but believes international funds will be better investments next year. Which international funds should she consider?
C|net	You would like to give your aunt an electronic dictionary software package. If price is not an issue, which one would you choose?
Disney	Which Walt Disney World hotel with access to the monorail would you choose to stay in?

Difficulty of Questions

We designed our test questions to be reasonably simple (so we could fit more of them into our test session) and to be about equally difficult for each site.

After browsing through each site, we came up with questions related to the content of the site. We tried not to make the answers too obvious (such as having the answer right on the home page), so the user would have to explore the site. On the other hand, we didn't want the questions to be so difficult that the user would give up.

Before bringing in real users, we held a rehearsal of our test questions using web-savvy people as users. Many of our questions proved to be harder than we originally anticipated — the rehearsal helped us identify questions that took an experienced web user more than about 10 or 15 minutes to answer. We modified or discarded questions as necessary until they met our goals.

Usability Testing Methodology

Since we were testing general-interest sites, we did not require the users in our study to have any particular skills or even a high degree of web proficiency. We did recruit people who were familiar with a web browser. The amount of web experience ranged from two weeks to two years, from less than one hour per week to more than four hours per day.

We brought users to our test facility for a three-hour test session, and each user tested as many web sites as possible in that time (no user tested all the sites). We varied the order in which the sites were tested so that we collected roughly the same amount of data on each site.

In our pre-test briefing, we told users that we would first take them to a web site, and then ask them to find the answers to several questions. We made it clear that the answers were always available somewhere within that site. We used Netscape Navigator's bookmarks to get users to each site, so users did not have to find out a site's URL or type it in.

We used Netscape Navigator 3.0 in our usability tests. Since we were not specifically testing web browsers and a couple of our users had minimal web browser experience, we did assist users with any browser-related difficulties (such as the use of bookmarks) that arose during the test. We did this so that users would not associate a specific site with a problem that actually pertained to the web browser.

While users worked, we minimized our interaction with them. We did not require them to use the classic usability testing "think aloud" approach, though we did record the things users said and did.

Data Collection

We counted a task as successful if the user found the right answer (for fact questions) or gave an answer he or she was comfortable with (for judgment questions). If the user gave an incorrect answer, couldn't find enough information to form an opinion, or gave up, we counted the task as unsuccessful.

Mid-Test Questionnaires

We also collected data after each task by means of a brief questionnaire, as shown in Figure 17.1. We used a format based on a method for workload studies developed at NASA. By measuring factors such as fatigue and confusion, we can put different sites on the same scale. In effect, these questions give us numerical data on the subjective experience the user has in working with the site.

The eighth question in this questionnaire (How would you have answered this question if you didn't have web access?) is an example of the type of question we use when we're not quite sure what we're looking for — just "fishing" for any interesting patterns we can find. In our testing, the eighth question didn't bring up any interesting patterns that we

FIGURE 17.1

POST-TASK QUESTIONS   S1T2

Please take a minute to answer the following questions.

1. **Physically, how do you feel right now?**

   exhausted   1   2   3   4   5   6   7   full of energy

2. **Mentally, how did you feel while working on this site?**

   completely
   confused   1   2   3   4   5   6   7   everything
                                            made sense

3. **While completing this task, did you**

   feel completely
   frustrated   1   2   3   4   5   6   7   always know what
                                              to do next

4. **Compared to what you expected, did this task go**

   much slower   1   2   3   4   5   6   7   much faster

5. **Rate the quality of information in this site.**

   unacceptable   1   2   3   4   5   6   7   excellent

6. **How confident are you that you found all the relevant information?**

   not at all
   confident   1   2   3   4   5   6   7   very
                                            confident

7. **How do you feel now that this task is over?**

   relieved   1   2   3   4   5   6   7   eager for more

8. **How would you have answered this question if you didn't have web access?**
   (Check all that apply.)

   ____ Read something (What? _____)

   ____ Called someone (Who? _____)

   ____ Gone somewhere (Where? _____)

   ____ Other: _____

FIGURE 17.1

Our mid-test questionnaire. We used the answers to questions 3, 4, and 6 to calculate the site rankings.

could discover in the sites. Some of the answers, however, might have been of interest to the designers of specific sites. Only in the case of C|net did users mention other alternatives on the Internet (news groups, AOL forum). All other alternate sources were either books (libraries) or personal references (people they could trust).

Calculating the Site Ratings

We could have rated the sites solely according to the percentage of questions the users got right, but then a good site might have done poorly if we happened to give it an unusually hard question. Fortunately, we found a better way to measure.

Answers to three of the mid-test questions (pertaining to how frustrated the user was while working with the site, the user's perception of how long the task took, and the user's confidence in the answer) were highly correlated with successful completion of the task, users' preferences, and other factors from the post-test questionnaire. We decided to use these three questions to calculate the site ratings.

For each site, we took the average answer to questions 3, 4, and 6 and multiplied them together. Since each question used a scale from 1 to 7, the highest possible rating a site could achieve was 7x7x7, or 343. We then divided the site's score by 343 to place it on a scale from 1 to 100.

Post-Test Questionnaires

After users had finished working with a site, we gave them a post-test questionnaire asking them to rate the site in 16 different areas. The questionnaire is shown in Figure 17.2. We asked users to put their answers for multiple sites on the same questionnaire, so they could see their own comparative judgments. We allowed users to modify answers after they'd seen other sites, though very few users chose to do so.

Web Site Main Study

User #____________

Date ____________

Post-Test Site Comparison

Please rate your satisfaction with the sites you have just finished working with. Put A for **Annuities,** C for **Car,** T for **Travel, and** O for **Olympics** on the scale to indicate your level of satisfaction.

1. Ease of finding specific information	very unsatisfied	1	2	3	4	5	6	7	very satisfied
2. Ease of reading data	very unsatisfied	1	2	3	4	5	6	7	very satisfied
3. Ease of concentrating on the data search (distractions)	very unsatisfied	1	2	3	4	5	6	7	very satisfied
4. Logic of navigation	very unsatisfied	1	2	3	4	5	6	7	very satisfied
5. Ease of search	very unsatisfied	1	2	3	4	5	6	7	very satisfied
6. Appearance of site	very unsatisfied	1	2	3	4	5	6	7	very satisfied
7. Quality of graphics	very unsatisfied	1	2	3	4	5	6	7	very satisfied
8. Relevance of graphics to site subject	very unsatisfied	1	2	3	4	5	6	7	very satisfied
9. Speed of data display	very unsatisfied	1	2	3	4	5	6	7	very satisfied
10. Timeliness of data (is it current?)	very unsatisfied	1	2	3	4	5	6	7	very satisfied
11. Quality of language	very unsatisfied	1	2	3	4	5	6	7	very satisfied
12. Fun to use?	very unsatisfied	1	2	3	4	5	6	7	very satisfied
13. Explanations of how to use site	very unsatisfied	1	2	3	4	5	6	7	very satisfied
14. Overall ease of use	very unsatisfied	1	2	3	4	5	6	7	very satisfied
15. Completeness with which the site's subject is treated	very unsatisfied	1	2	3	4	5	6	7	very satisfied
16. Your overall productivity with the site	very unsatisfied	1	2	3	4	5	6	7	very satisfied

FIGURE 17.2

Our post-test questionnaire. Users rated all the sites they tested on the same page.

Post-Test Questionnaire Results

From all the users' questionnaires, we obtained a comparative picture of the nine sites. Table 17.5 shows how users rated the individual sites in each of these areas. The sites are arranged left to right from best to worst according to our rankings.

TABLE 17.5

Summary of post-test data for all sites. The numbers are the average of all responses from the users who tested the site.

	Edmund's	Olympic	Hewlett Packard	WebSaver	Travelocity	Inc. (new)	C|net	Fidelity	Inc. (old)	Disney (new)	Disney (old)
1. Ease of finding specific information	5.36	6.33	5.67	5.08	5.08	5.50	3.64	3.50	3.80	4.00	4.00
2. Ease of reading data	5.55	6.67	5.92	5.31	5.69	6.50	4.55	5.33	5.00	4.27	5.25
3. Ease of concentrating on the data search (distractions)	5.27	5.33	5.08	5.77	5.15	4.50	4.00	3.67	4.60	4.73	5.00
4. Logic of navigation	5.55	5.33	5.42	5.15	5.31	5.50	4.00	3.83	4.40	4.27	4.25
5. Ease of search	4.82	5.33	5.67	5.00	5.15	6.00	3.82	3.67	3.80	4.00	3.75
6. Appearance of site	4.64	6.00	5.92	4.92	5.08	5.50	4.09	4.67	5.00	5.73	5.25
7. Quality of graphics	4.36	5.67	6.00	4.92	4.92	4.00	4.10	4.50	4.60	5.91	5.25
8. Relevance of graphics to site subject	5.18	6.00	6.00	4.54	4.92	4.50	4.45	5.00	4.40	5.82	5.00
9. Speed of data display	5.09	6.00	4.33	5.15	3.92	5.50	5.00	4.67	4.80	4.91	5.50
10. Timeliness of data (is it current?)	6.27	6.00	5.75	5.23	5.54	6.00	5.27	5.83	4.70	5.91	5.25
11. Quality of language	5.91	5.33	6.00	5.08	5.69	6.00	4.91	5.80	4.80	5.82	5.00
12. Fun to use?	5.00	6.00	5.00	3.83	5.00	4.00	3.73	4.83	3.20	5.00	4.00
13. Explanations of how to use site	4.64	5.00	4.92	4.31	4.50	5.00	3.82	3.67	3.80	4.55	4.25
14. Overall ease of use	5.45	6.00	5.42	5.08	5.15	5.00	4.09	3.83	4.20	4.64	4.50
15. Completeness with which the site's subject is treated	5.64	5.00	6.17	4.46	5.15	5.00	4.09	4.67	4.60	5.09	4.75
16. Your overall productivity with the site	4.91	5.33	5.33	5.08	5.23	4.50	3.82	4.00	4.00	4.64	3.75

How Good Is Good Enough?

The definition of "usability" for a particular web site depends on what the organization expects it to accomplish. For an internal human resources web site, fun and entertainment are probably not part of the site's goals. However, "surfing" may be extremely important for a site like Disney. Conversely, looking up specific facts might be the top priority for the human resources site and not as crucial for Disney.

Our study allowed us to compare our test sites against each other, but we did not attempt to determine what constitutes "good enough" for any of these sites. We cannot say that any of these sites is better or worse than the others, because we don't have information about what their developers were trying to accomplish. We can't judge any web site as good or bad unless we design and conduct usability tests based on a thorough knowledge of its goals.

When we test web sites for usability in our client work, we ask two questions: "What are the obstacles to the users accomplishing their goals?" and "What do we change to remove those obstacles?" That way, we ensure that we are focusing our efforts on those areas that are most important to users, and thus to the success of the site.

User Interface Engineering

User Interface Engineering is a consulting firm specializing in product usability and design. Our mission is to empower product development teams to build applications that meet the needs of their users by providing critical data for decision making. To fulfill this mission, we combine three activities:

- **Consulting**
  We work directly with development teams who want to produce more usable products. Our consulting projects provide us with a wealth of insights about what actually works in the real world.

- **Training**
  We offer several public and corporate courses to teach what we've learned about effective design and the methods we've found successful in our research and consulting work. We also give short presentations, including a talk based on this report.

- **Research**

  We conduct original research on aspects of product usability. In addition to this web site study, we have also studied wizards in commercial software, and we plan to conduct additional research studies on other areas of interface design.

Additional Resources

Here are some ways to learn about User Interface Engineering's latest findings from our research and consulting work.

Eye For Design Newsletter

Six times a year, we publish *Eye For Design*, a newsletter containing articles about product design and development. *Eye For Design* articles come from our real-world experience of what works and what doesn't. Previous issues have included articles on:

- Pitfalls of Installation Programs
- When to Develop a Wizard
- Harnessing the Power of User Myths
- Why On-Site Searching Stinks
- The 3 Roles of the Usability Test Facilitator
- Designing for the Right Audience
- Online Help: Sometimes It Doesn't Help

To receive a free issue or to subscribe, visit our web site or give us a call.

UIEtips E-mail Publication

UIEtips is a free e-mail publication that focuses on all aspects of product usability. **UIETips** subscribers receive up-to-date information on the results of our latest research and consulting work, including special offers on new courses, publications, and services. To subscribe, send an e-mail message to UIETips-Request@uie.com. The body of the message should say subscribe.

User Interface Engineering Web Site

The User Interface Engineering web site at www.uie.com includes *Eye For Design* articles, descriptions and schedules for our public courses, and other information on our products and services.

Contact Information

User Interface Engineering
800 Turnpike Street, Suite 101
North Andover, MA 01845
Phone: (978) 975-4343
Fax: (978) 975-5353
E-mail: uie@uie.com
http://www.uie.com

If you have comments or questions or would like to be added to our mailing list, please feel free to contact us.